FASHION & COSMETICS GRAPHICS

P·I·E BOOKS

FASHION & COSMETICS GRAPHICS

First published in Japan 1995 by:
P·I·E BOOKS
#301 4-14-6, Komagome, Toshima-ku, Tokyo 170, Japan
TEL: 03-3949-5010 FAX: 03-3949-5650

ISBN4-938586-50-9 C3070 P16000E

First Published in Germany 1995 by:
NIPPAN / Nippon Shuppan Hanbai Deutschland GmbH
Krefelder Str. 85, D-40549, Düsserdolf, Germany
TEL: 0211-5048089 FAX: 0211-5049326

ISBN3-910052-39-8

Printed in Hong Kong by Everbest Printing Co., Ltd.

CONTENTS

EDITORIAL NOTES:

CD: Creative Director
AD: Art Director
D: Designer
P: Photographer
I: Illustrator
CW: Copywriter
DF: Design Firm

クレジット中、年度は発表
年度を表記しています。

The year indicated is the
year of launch.

はじめに

　ファッション界とグラフィック・デザインの位置関係は、理想的なパター
ンといえるかもしれない。――そう思ったのは、他の様々な業界でのクライ
アントと広告制作者との関係を見た時に、両者のバランスがうまく取れてい
ないケースが多々あるような気がしたからだ。クライアントの意志ばかりが
強く反映されて、消費者の目に止まりにくい広告や、デザインばかりが先行
して、クライアントの意志が見えてこない広告ができ上がってしまう――そ
んな中で、ファッションとグラフィック・デザインは両者が同一の位置にい
て、触発しあって関係をつないでいるような印象を強く受ける。

　例えばファッションと対モデル、対フォトグラファーの関係を思うとわか
りやすいかもしれない。彼らはファッションを引き立てる役目をしながらも、
同時にファッションに対し十∂を与え、その結果、より魅力的な見せ方を生
んでいる。双方がコラボレートして、ひとつのイメージをつくりあげる――
それがグラフィック・デザインにも浸透してきているような気がするのだ。

　本書にはカタログに始まり、ダイレクト・メール、ポスター、ＰＯＰ、パ
ッケージ類や店舗のデザインまで作品が幅広く掲載されているが、そのどれ
にも先述の「理想的な関係」がゆき届いている。ファッションの持つパワー、
そして、それを限りなく表現するグラフィック・デザインの良さが、きっと
あなたにも素直に感じ取れるはずだ。

　ソニア・リキエルの香水" Le parfum "のプレス用資料中にこんな言葉が
あった。「無理にひとつに統一してしまうのではなく、相反するもの同士、
バランスをとりながら共存していく…これが90年代の生き方、『対比するも
のの調和』なのです」。

　クライアントとクリエイターとの結びつきと調和。人々を引き付ける広告
を作り上げるための第一歩は、ここにあるのではないだろうか。

P·I·E BOOKS

Foreword

It may just be that the fashion world and purveyors of graphic design have achieved that elusive ideal - a perfectly balanced relationship. We have reached this conclusion after observing the working relationship between clients in all sorts of other lines of business and their creative teams, and finding many cases where balance is lacking. For instance, some advertisements concentrate heavily on the client's requirements and in doing so sacrifice their appeal to the consumer, while others lead off strongly on design and virtually ignore the wishes of the client. But with the fashion world, we get the impression that not only do fashion and graphic design maintain a healthy equilibrium in this respect, but both sides get a powerful spark from their fortuitous contact.

This is perhaps easier to understand if we think in terms of the relation to fashion of models, for instance, or photographers. The role of both is obviously to enhance the fashion they are helping to display, but at the same time they undoubtedly supply some indefinable 'plus alpha' that leads to a more attactive end result. It is the effective collaboration they have with the fashion world that produces the final image, and this seems to be the formula widely used in graphic design.

This book features artwork for a vast range of different advertising media, starting with catalogues and including direct mail, posters, point-of-purchase display, packaging and boutique design, and in every case the 'ideally balanced relationship' is plainly evident. For the reader, this collection puts across the power inherent in fashion as well as the unbounded quality of graphic design used for its portrayal.

A press release on Sonia Rykiel's 'Le Parfum' refers to the 1990s as the time for a live-and-let-live lifestyle, balancing those factors that pull in different directions rather than pressuring them into any sort of conformity... a time to create harmony out of contrasting or even conflicting factors.

We have come to think that harmonization of this type between client and creative team may perhaps be the first ingredient needed to produce advertising that will truly captivate the public.

P·I·E BOOKS

Vorwort

Ein kaum zu fassendes Ideal könnte erreicht worden sein: Die perfekt ausgewogene Beziehung zwischen der Modewelt und den für sie arbeitenden Graphik-Designern. Wir kommen zu diesem Schluß, nachdem wir die Arbeitsbeziehungen zwischen Kunden in allen möglichen Branchen und den für sie arbeitenden Kreativen kennengelernt haben und dabei in vielen Fällen eine mangelnde Ausgewogenheit fanden. Zum Beispiel konzentrieren sich einige Anzeigen ganz stark auf die Anforderungen der Auftraggeber. Indem sie dies tun, verlieren sie stark an Attraktivität für den Endverbraucher. Im Gegensatz dazu konzentrieren sich andere sehr stark auf Design und ignorieren dabei die Anforderungen des Auftraggebers. In der Modewelt scheint unseres Eindruckes nach nicht nur ein gesundes Gleichgewicht zwischen Auftraggebern und Graphik-Designern zu herrschen, sondern beide Seiten bekommen offensichtlich kräftige Impulse aus ihren jeweiligen gegenseitigen Kontakten.

Dies ist wahrscheinlich leichter zu verstehen, wenn wir die Beziehungen vergleichen, in denen die Mode zu den Models steht oder auch zu den Mode-Photographen. Die Rolle von beiden ist es offensichtlich, den Eindruck der Mode, die sie helfen zu zeigen, zu verstärken. Gleichzeitig produzieren sie einen undefinierbaren "plus alpha-Faktor", der einen attraktiveren Verkaufserfolg bewirkt. Die effektive Zusammenarbeit, die sie mit der Modewelt haben, bestimmt das endgültige Image - und dieses Muster scheint auch für das Graphik-Design Gültigkeit zu haben.

Das hier vorliegende Buch zeigt Arbeiten für eine große Zahl von verschiedenen Werbemitteln, angefangen mit Katalogen und anderen Direct Mail-Stücken über Poster, Point-of-Purchase Displays und Packungen bis hin zu Boutiquen-Designs. In jedem Fall ist die geschilderte "ideal ausgewogene Beziehung" evident. Für den Betrachter wird durch diese Sammlung die Kraft spürbar, die in der Mode selbst steckt, wie auch die anscheinend grenzenlose Qualität des Graphik-Design, das die Mode porträtiert.

Eine Presseinformation über Sonia Rykiels "Le Parfum" definiert die 90er Jahre als die Zeit für den "leben-und-leben-lassen" Lebensstil. Dieser balanciert all jene Faktoren, die nach verschiedenen Richtungen streben, als daß er versucht, sie in eine Art von Konformität zu pressen - eine Zeit, in der Harmonie aus kontrastierenden oder selbst im Konflikt stehenden Faktoren geschaffen wird.

Wir denken deshalb, daß eine Harmonisierung dieser Art zwischen Klienten und Kreativteams vielleicht die erste benötigte Ingredienz ist, um Werbung zu produzieren, die das Publikum wirklich in Bann zieht.

P·I·E BOOKS

Clothes

SONIA RYKIEL
PARIS

SONIA RYKIEL
PARIS

Sonia Rykiel

Designer: Sonia Rykiel
Country of original launch: France
Year of launch: 1968
Coverage: women's apparel / accessories

Sonia Rykiel invents fashion from one day to the next. She loves clothes that go together, that play together, that are organized together, but also clothes that shine and sparkle.

ソニア・リキエルは次から次へと新しいファッションを創案。バランスのとれた服の組み合わせや、楽しい服の取り合わせ、トータルにコーディネートされたファッションを得意とする一方で、きらめきのある華やかな服にも強く興味を抱いている

Postcard; Spring-Summer 1993; D: Sonia Rykiel P: Peter Lindbergh

Packages / bags / ribbon

+ 12 Sonia Rykiel

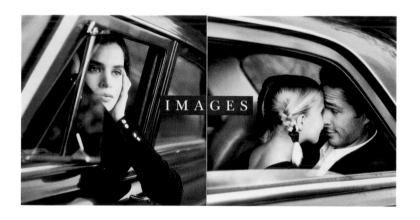

6, rue de Grenelle

SONIA RYKIEL

PARIS

+ 14 Sonia Rykiel

Plain, striped and ribbed, knitted jackets with bras or nothing underneath. Soft tailoring in wool crepe, jersey, and linen, herringbones and checks. Long jackets, tunics in crepe viscose, narrow fitted shapes, shorts, long skirts and wide trousers. For fun, double knitted oversized cardigans. Split cotton dresses and vibrant prints. A woman who inspires perfume enjoys herself.

Postcards / invitation cards / greeting cards; 1991-1994; D, I: Sonia Rykiel

Sonia Rykiel **15**

Publicity item / notebook; D, I: Sonia Rykiel

Greeting card; 1990-1991; D, I: Sonia Rykiel

RYKIEL
HOMME

Rykiel Homme

Designer: Sonia Rykiel
Country of original launch: France
Year of launch: 1990
Coverage: men's apparel / accessories

Men's fashion to complement Sonia Rykiel's women's label.
Men who wear Rykiel Homme value its authenticity, comfortable
cut and all-round attention to detail.

Sonia Rykiel を着た女性にふさわしい男の服 ——**Rykiel Homme**。
このファッションを着こなす男たちは、あらゆる部分において、
ささいなディティールやオーセンティックなもの、気持ち良さを
大事にしている。

Leaflet; Autumn-Winter 1994; D: Sonia Rykiel

Rykiel Homme   17

Notebook; D, I: Sonia Rykiel

Postcards; 1991-1994; D: Sonia Rykiel P: Peter Lindbergh / Jacques Olivar

Lolita Lempicka

Designer: Lolita Lempicka
Country of original launch: France
Year of launch: 1983
Coverage: women's apparel

A label based on the concept of classic elegance, featuring design that uses flowery prints and lace to accentuate women's inherent attractiveness and femininity.

「クラシックなエレガンス」がコンセプト。花柄のプリントや
レース等を使用したデザインは、女性特有のかわいらしさと
セクシーさを感じさせる。

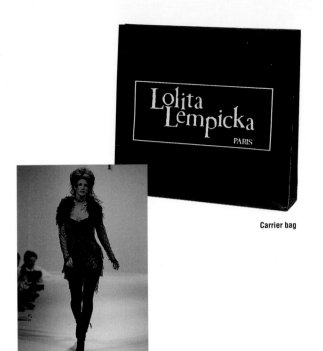

Carrier bag

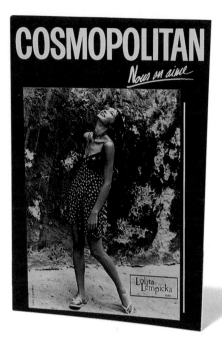

POP display

Magazine ad; AD, I: Michel Charrier

Invitation card; Autumn-Winter 1994-1995; AD, I: Michel Charrier

KRIZIA

Krizia

Designer: Mariuccia Mandelli
Country of original launch: Italy
Year of launch: 1954
Coverage: men's, women's, casual apparel /
accessories / cosmetics / perfume

Versatile fashion to match people's diversified lifestyles and the
latest directions in environmental and cultural issues. Optional
themes feature animals and fine art, for delicately and imaginatively
designed clothes.

人々の多用なライフスタイル、環境・文化の発展などと共に歩む
応用性の高いファッションであり、自由な選択ができるような
デザイン、テーマが動物だったり、芸術からの引用と、
様々な創造力と繊細さがあふれている。

Carrier bag / packages

KRIZIA

Brochure; Spring-Summer 1995; P: Patrick Demarchelier

I TONI, I COLORI, I DISEGNI DELLE STAGIONI.

RUBATI.

STAGIONI
by
KRIZIA

Brochure; Spring-Summer 1993; P: Giovanni Gastel

Magazine ad; Autumn-Winter 1994; P: Helmut Newton

Krazy Krazy Krazy Krizia.

KRAZY
KRIZIA

Brochure; Autumn-Winter 1992; P: Giovanni Gastel

Brochure; Autumn-Winter 1992; P: Giovanni Gastel

Daniel Jasiak
composition indéfinie:

P: Yutaka Yamamoto

A Istambul,
j'ai planté quelques arbustes.
En Australie, j'ai déposé ma violence.
Plié, tourmenté, creé, brûlé.
Point par point. Tout avec les mains.
Pour beaucoup d'amour.
Avec beaucoup d'éclats au regard des autres,
Voler en éclats avant d'être coupé.
Assembler avant d'être coupé.
Ne pas pleurer. Silence, il y a bonheur.
Infiniment mal fait.
Des corps mal construits.
L'expérience de Calcutta.
Affronter l'impossible.
Et puis le passé, le présent déjà passé,
Et présent. Recommencer encore.
Modifier l'inconnu avec une sensibilité.
Des tissus marqués, périmés, tâches,
déchirés, oubliés.
Try to touch me if you can,
Jeux de sensation pour vêtements
qui vous connaissent.
Trahir tous les patrons.
With love.

Daniel Jasiak
composition indéfinie

Tag label

Daniel Jasiak

Designer: Daniel Jasiak
Country of original launch: France
Year of launch: 1984
Coverage: women's apparel

Daniel Jasiak is attracting attention for his 'recycled fashion'.
His make-overs of existing garments by adding contrasting
fabrics demonstrate his love of dress-making.

パリで話題を集めたリサイクル・ファッションの流れと共に、
注目を浴び始めた**Daniel Jasiak**。パターンを作らず、既成の服を
思うままに他の布と縫い合わせて仕上げるファッションからは、
作り手の、洋服への深い愛情を感じ取ることができる。

P: Yutaka Yamamoto

27 Daniel Jasiak

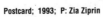

Postcard

Postcard; 1993; P: Zia Ziprin

KATHARINE HAMNETT LONDON

(bottom) Publicity item; Autumn-Winter 1990; CD: Katharine Hamnett P: Ellen von Unwerth

28

Katharine Hamnett London

Designer: Katharine Hamnett
Country of original launch: England
Year of launch: 1979
Coverage: men's, women's, casual apparel / accessories

Not just sexy, not just intelligent and classy, also refreshingly new.
Noticed for always being the trend-setter, Katherine Hamnett fashion
is nonetheless ageless, up-to-the-minute and universal.

セクシーでありながらもインテリジェンス、クラシックで
ありながらも新しい。キャサリン・ハムネットのデザインは、
常にトレンドの仕掛け役として注目を浴びているが、時代性を
超え、今やファッションの普遍的な要素になり得ている。

POP display; Autumn-Winter 1994; P: Juergen Teller

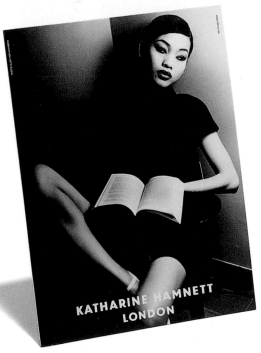

POP display; Spring-Summer 1995; P: Ellen von Unwerth

POP display; Autumn-Winter 1994; P: Juergen Teller

KATHARINE HAMNETT
LONDON

KATHARINE HAMNETT
LONDON

Magazine ad; Spring-Summer 1994;
CD: Katharine Hamnett P: Juergen Teller

KATHARINE HAMNETT

Brochure; Spring-Summer 1992; P: Ellen von Unwerth

HIROKO KOSHINO

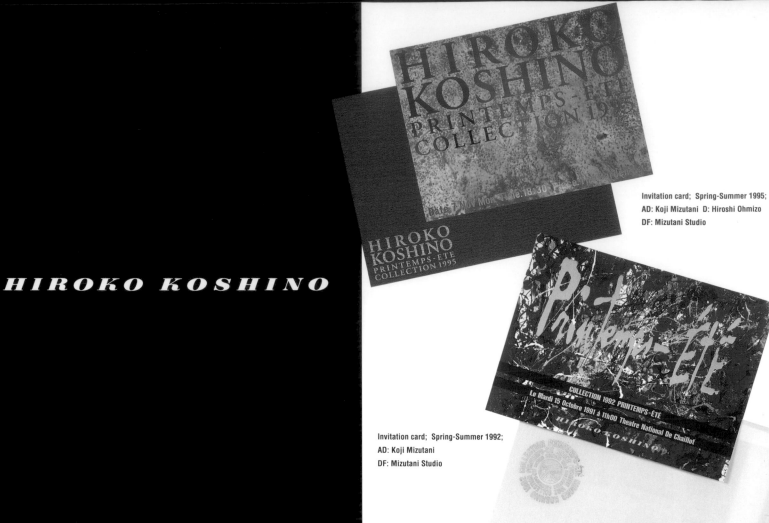

Invitation card; Spring-Summer 1995;
AD: Koji Mizutani D: Hiroshi Ohmizo
DF: Mizutani Studio

Invitation card; Spring-Summer 1992;
AD: Koji Mizutani
DF: Mizutani Studio

Hiroko Koshino

Designer: Hiroko Koshino　コシノ ヒロコ
Country of original launch: Japan
Year of launch: 1982
Coverage: women's apparel / accessories

The theme of the Hiroko Koshino '95-'96 autumn / winter collection is
'over-laying'. A fusion of fresh, modern ideas onto inspiration taken
from the enduring world of timeless tradition.

'95〜'96 ヒロコ コシノ秋冬コレクションは "over-lay" がテーマ。
時代を超えて生きつづける伝統の世界をインスピレーション・
ソースに、鮮度の高いモダンなアイデアを融合させている。

Brochure; Autumn-Winter 1991; AD: Koji Mizutani D: Hiroshi Ohmizo P: Katsuo Hanzawa DF: Mizutani Studio

Poster; 1990; AD: Koji Mizutani
P: Yoshihiko Ueda DF: Mizutani Studio

Poster; 1991; AD: Koji Mizutani
D: Hiroshi Ohmizo P: Katsuo Hanzawa
DF: Mizutani Studio

Poster; 1992; AD: Koji Mizutani
D: Hiroshi Ohmizo P: Sachiko Kuru
DF: Mizutani Studio

Brochure; Autumn-Winter 1993; AD: Koji Mizutani D: Hiroshi Ohmizo P: Katsuo Hanzawa DF: Mizutani Studio

Hiroko Koshino 35

Brochure; Autumn-Winter 1990; AD: Koji Mizutani P: Kazuyasu Hagane DF: Mizutani Studio

MOSCHINO

X YEARS OF KAOS !

1983　1984　1985　1986

1987　1988　1989　1990

STOP THE FASHION SYSTEM !

...and me ?

I ♥ DRUGS !

?

1991　1992　1993　1994

THE EXHIBITION
September 16th October 21st 1993
Milan Museo della Permanente via Turati 34

MOSCHINO

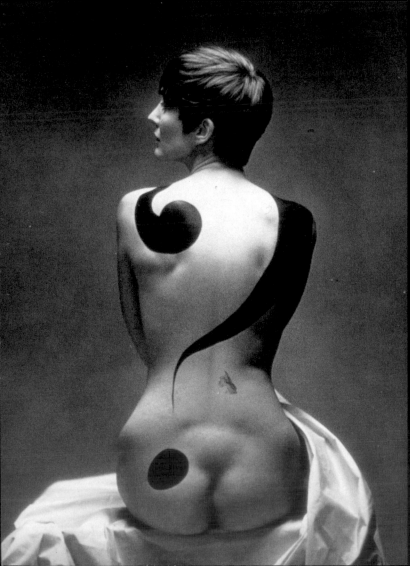

Moschino

Designer: Rossella Jardini
Country of original launch: Italy
Year of launch: 1983
Coverage: men's, women's, children's, casual apparel /
accessories / perfume

Unconventional clothes designed with wit and humour that are great
to wear. Multiple co-ordinating alternatives produce a personalized
look. Well produced clothes with an ageless, universal appeal.

常識にとらわれず、ウィットやユーモアに富み、着る人を幸せに
するような服。コーディネーションの可能性が多岐にわたり、
それによりパーソナリティをも引き出す。服作りの基礎が
しっかりとした、時代を越え、普遍性のある服である。

Moschino 37

Invitation card / direct mail material; 1986-1995; AD: Franco Moschino

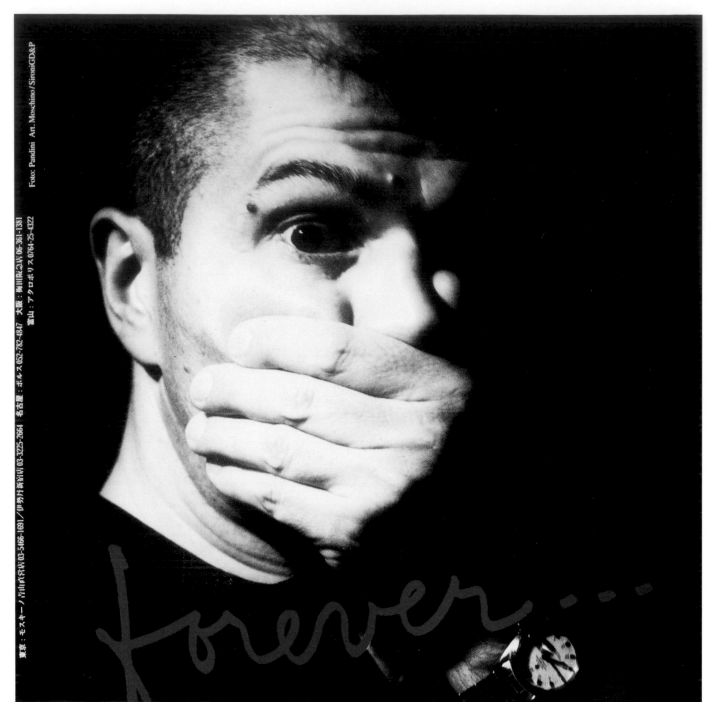

forever...

MOSCHINO

Publicity item; Spring-Summer 1995; AD: Franco Moschino P: S. Pandini

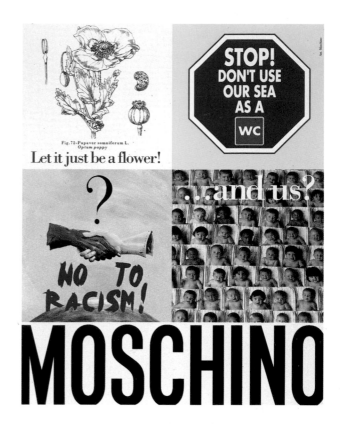

Moschino 39

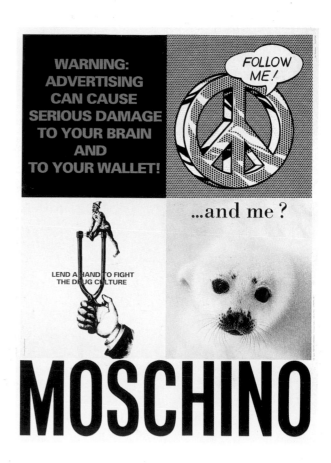

40 Moschino

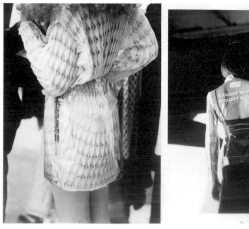

Brochure; Autumn-Winter 1994-1995; AD: Franco Moschino

GUESS

Guess?

Country of original launch: USA
Year of launch: 1981
Coverage: men's, women's, children's, casual apparel / accessories

Launched in 1981 with one jean silhouette - the sleek Marilyn 3-zip -
Guess? today is a total lifestyle collection. Guess? wardrobes men,
women and children in a casual but elegant style.

1981年、ジーンズ・ファッション "the Sleek Marilyn 3-zip" を
発表して以来、**Guess?**は今日トータルなライフスタイルを
演出するコレクションに成長を遂げている。メンズ、
レディースそして子供服にいたるワードローブは、カジュアル
かつエレガントなスタイルを確立している。

Self-adhesive notes; 1991; AD: Paul Marciano D: Samantha Gibson
P: Ellen von Unwerth / Neil Kirk / Dominick Guillemot DF: Guess?, Inc.

Gift stationery folder / pencil set / address book; 1991; AD: Paul Marciano
D: Samantha Gibson P: Ellen von Unwerth / Neil Kirk CW: Emily Corey DF: Guess?, Inc.

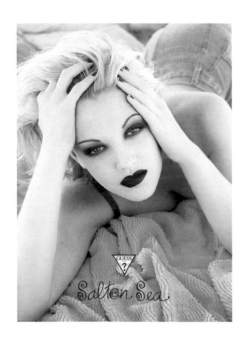

Brochure; 1993; CD, AD: Paul Marciano D: Leslie Oki P: Wayne Maser CW: Emily Corey DF: Guess? Advertising

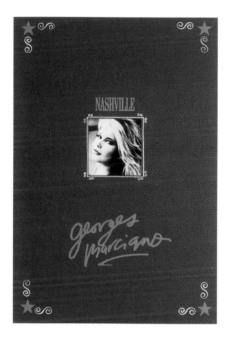

Brochure; 1989; CD, AD: Paul Marciano P: Ellen von Unwerth CW: Emily Corey DF: Guess? Advertising

MAY

SUN	MON	TUE	WED	THU	FRI	SAT
	1	2	3	4	5	6
7	8	9	10	11	12	13
14	15	16	17	18	19	20
21	22	23	24	25	26	27
28	29	30	31			

APRIL

SUN	MON	TUE	WED	THU	FRI	SAT
						1
2	3	4	5	6	7	8
9	10	11	12	13	14	15
16	17	18	19	20	21	22
23	24	25	26	27	28	29
30						

**1995
CALENDAR**

MAURICE MARCIANO
PAUL MARCIANO
ARMAND MARCIANO

OCTOBER

SUN	MON	TUE	WED	THU	FRI	SAT
1	2	3	4	5	6	7
8	9	10	11	12	13	14
15	16	17	18	19	20	21
22	23	24	25	26	27	28
29	30	31				

JUNE

SUN	MON	TUE	WED	THU	FRI	SAT
				1	2	3
4	5	6	7	8	9	10
11	12	13	14	15	16	17
18	19	20	21	22	23	24
25	26	27	28	29	30	

Guess? 47

FEBRUARY

SUN	MON	TUE	WED	THU	FRI	SAT
		1	2	3	4	5
6	7	8	9	10	11	12
13	14	15	16	17	18	19
20	21	22	23	24	25	26
27	28					

JANUARY

SUN	MON	TUE	WED	THU	FRI	SAT
						1
2	3	4	5	6	7	8
9	10	11	12	13	14	15
16	17	18	19	20	21	22
23	24	25	26	27	28	29
30	31					

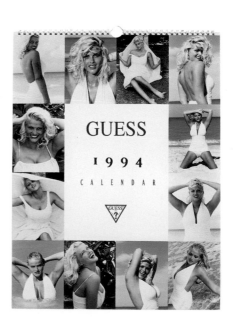

**GUESS
1994
CALENDAR**

Brochure; 1993; CD, AD: Paul Marciano D: Samantha Osselaer P: Neil Kirk CW: Emily Corey DF: Guess? Advertising

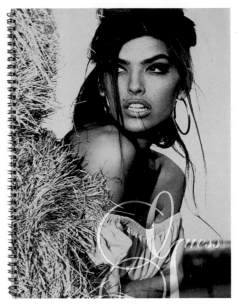

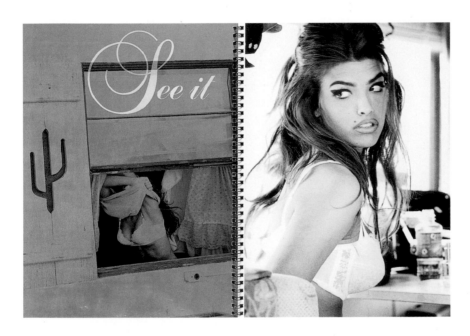

Guess? **+**

Brochure; 1991; CD, AD: Paul Marciano D: Samantha Osselaer P: Ellen von Unwerth CW: Emily Corey DF: Guess? Advertising

Paul Smith

Paul Smith

Designer: Paul Smith
Country of original launch: England
Year of launch: 1970
Coverage: men's, women's, children's, casual apparel / accessories

Clothes from the Paul Smith label are essentially down to earth.
An unexpected twist to traditional Englishman's styling produces a
'modern classic' look.

down-to-earth をポリシーとして服作りを続けているポール・スミス。
イギリスの伝統的メンズ・ファッションの中に、思いもかけない
ひとひねりを加える事で、モダン・クラシックの
流れを作り出している。

Promotional matches

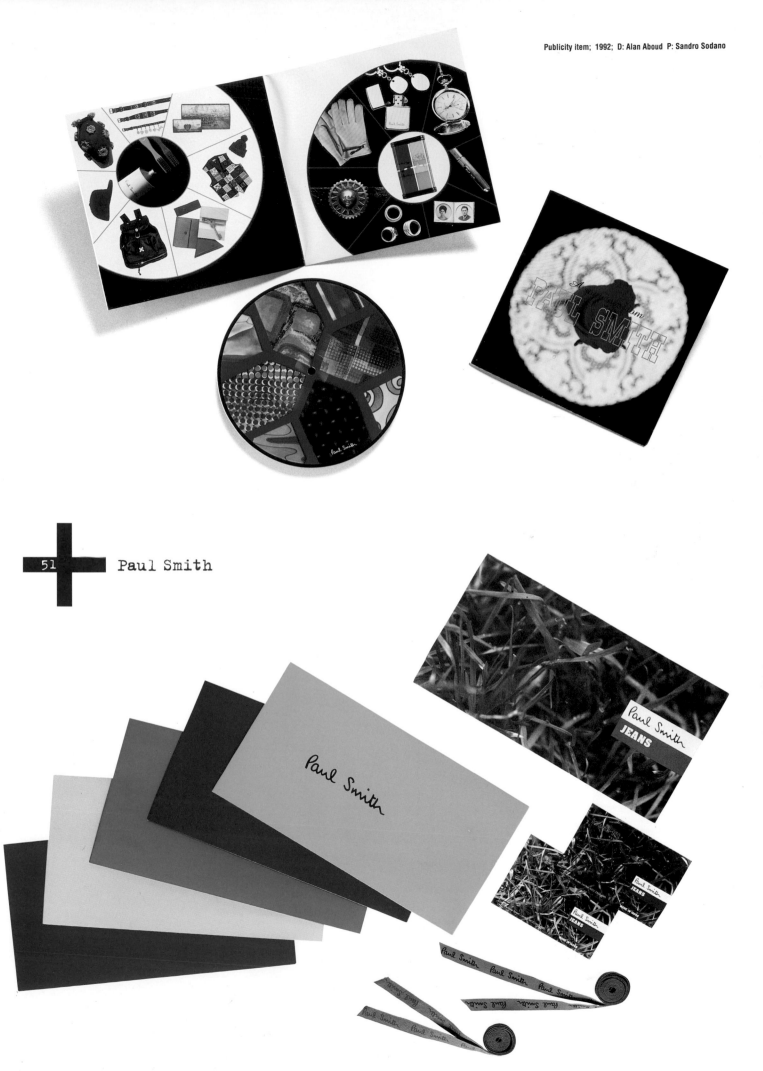

Publicity item; 1992; D: Alan Aboud P: Sandro Sodano

51 ✛ Paul Smith

Bag / ribbon / business card

52 Paul Smith

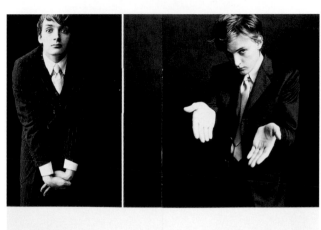

Paul Smith 53

paul SMITH
autumn•winter 1994

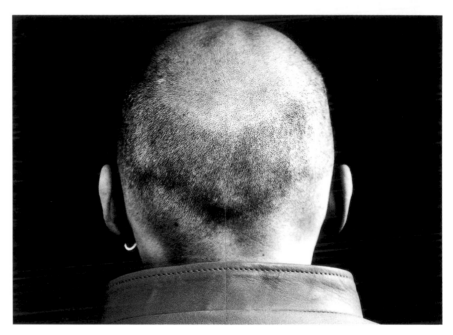

Brochure; Autumn - Winter 1994; AD, D: Alan Aboud P: David Bailey

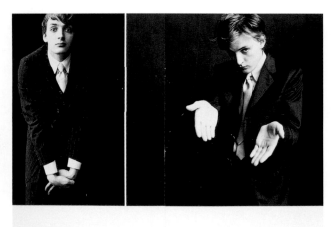

Paul Smith 53

paul SMITH
autumn•winter 1994

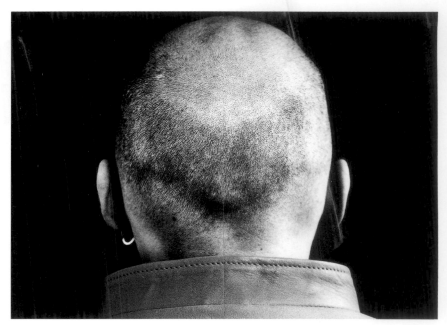

Brochure; Autumn - Winter 1994; AD, D: Alan Aboud P: David Bailey

56 Paul Smith

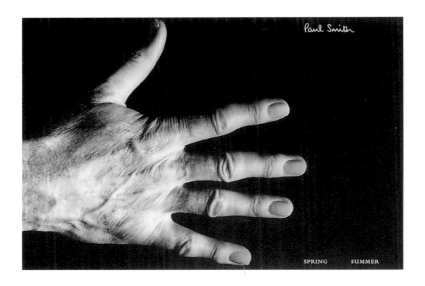

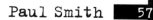

Paul Smith 57

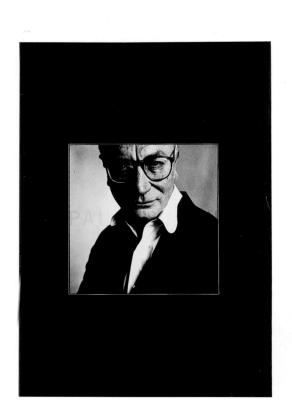

R. NEWBOLD

DAY SHIRT — soft collar, in 1890, patents were noted for a shirt that opens down the entire front so that it could be put on like a coat

DAYSHIRT

R. Newbold

Designer: Paul Smith
Country of original launch: England
Year of launch: 1993
Coverage: men's, casual apparel / accessories

Paul Smith took over the 1885-established Robert Brewster Newbold label in 1991. This "100% Genuine" label offers two contrasting styles of traditional Newbold items and Paul Smith's updated lines.

1885年に創業されたロバート・ブリュースター・ニューボールドの
ブランドを、約1世紀後の1991年にポール・スミスが受け継ぎ、
リニューアルさせたブランド。"100%本物"をモットーに、
かつての製品を元に表現した商品群＝コア・アイテムと、
ニューボールドのデザインにポール・スミスがモダンな味つけを
施したノンコア・アイテムの、ふたつの雰囲気が楽しめる。

Tags / envelopes / woven labels;

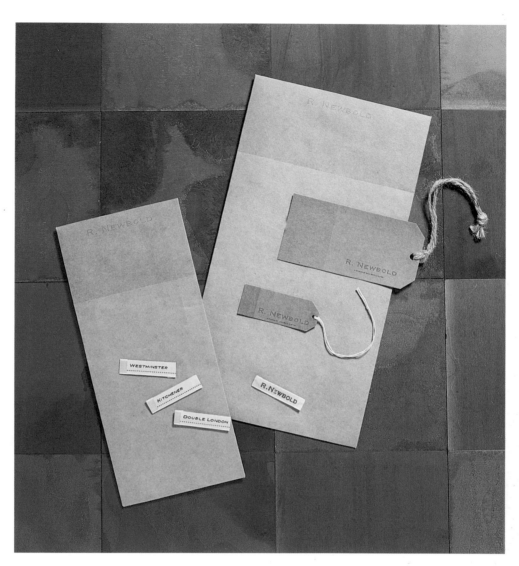

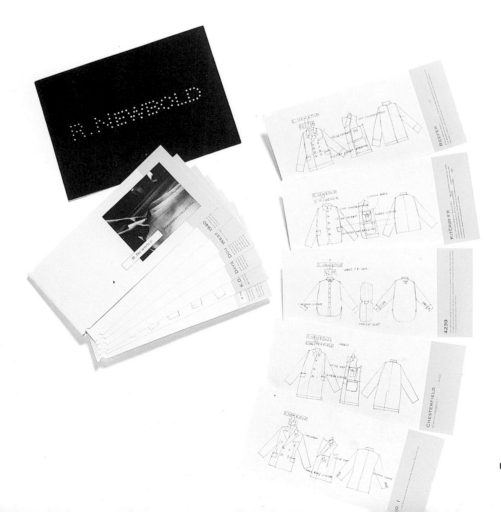

R. Newbold 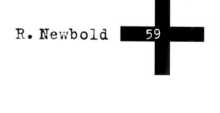 59

Publicity item / direct mail material; AD: Alan Aboud P: Sandro Sodano

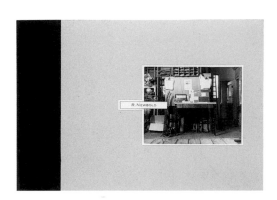

Brochure; AD: Alan Aboud P: Sandro Sodano

Brochure; Autumn-Winter 1994; AD: Alan Aboud P: Julian Broad

R. Newbold   63

TAKÉO KIKUCHI

Just Shirts Fair 4.7ᵗʰ-16

Takéo Kikuchi

Designer: Takeo Kikuchi　菊池武夫
Country of original launch: Japan
Year of launch: 1984
Coverage: men's apparel

Takeo Kikuchi applies current fashion trends to the long-established principles of men's outfitting. A brand of menswear that harmonizes classicism and modernism.

男性服飾の長い歴史の中で培われた基本をあくまで
大切にしながらも、菊池武夫というフィルターを通して
時代の気分を積極的に反映してゆく、クラシシズムと
モダニズムの調和を追及したブランド。

Poster; Spring-Summer 1995; D: Yoshinori Yamanaka P: Bruno

TAKÉO
KIKUCHI

Direct mail material; Autumn-Winter 1993; D: Yoshinori Yamanaka P: M. Hasui

Takéo Kikuchi   67

Direct mail material; Spring-Summer 1993;
D: Shintaro Abe P: M. Hasui

68 Takéo Kikuchi

Direct mail material; Autumn-Winter 1992;
D: Shintaro Abe P: M. Hasui

Poster; Autumn-Winter 1994; P: Sheila Metzner

5351 POUR LES HOMMES
et LES FEMMES

Gift bandanna / postcards / tags;
CD: Hideshi Maruya I: Junko Sakuraba

5351 Pour Les Hommes et Les Femmes

Designer: Hideshi Maruya   丸屋秀之
Country of original launch: Japan
Year of launch: 1993 (Hommes) / 1994 (Femmes)
Coverage: men's, women's apparel

Hommes stresses harmonized dressing, and a masculine, slightly
unrefined look inspired by the designer's lifestyle. Femmes is the
corresponding women's line. Clothes distinctive in their line,
detailing and fabric.

服と服のハーモニーを大切に、デザイナー自身のライフ・スタイル
から生まれる男ぼく、少し不良くさいスタイルの "Hommes"。
"Hommes"を着る男性の理想とする女性のスタイルが "Femmes"。
素材やディテール、シルエットにこだわる服。

Brochure; Autumn-Winter 1994-1995; CD: Hideshi Maruya
AD: Gyo Suzuki P: Winston Tatsukawa

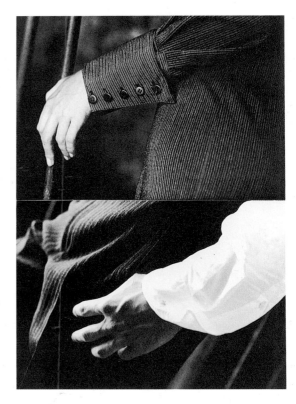

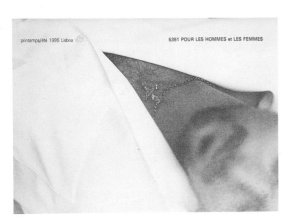

Brochure; Spring-Summer 1995; CD: Hideshi Maruya
AD: Gyo Suzuki P: Winston Tatsukawa

WILLY BOGNER PRESENTS

FIRE·AND·ICE

CLOTHING COMPANY

...D WITH FOUR SNOWBOARD-DAYS. WE
...ER RODE BEFORE. I DIDN'T KNOW THAT
...AND, AND WHAT WE FOUND WAS A HUGE
...ND LONG FACES. THE LOCALS GAVE US
...D, FULL THROTTLE AND YOU ALREADY
...NG THESE MOUNTAINS WAS A SPECIAL
...E THESE MOUNTAINS WERE STILL
...OME HOLES. IT WAS LIKE I DREAMT

Fire & Ice

Designer: Willy Bogner
Country of original launch: Germany
Coverage: Casual apparel

Outdoor fashion by Willy Bogner, of ski-wear fame, sporting the
watchword 'The Global Adventure'. A label dedicated to the great
outdoors and the young people who enjoy it.

スキー・ウェアで知られるウィリー・ボグナーの
アウトドア・ファッション。広告物のテーマになっている
"the global adventure" の言葉どおり、自然と、
それを楽しむ若者たちがこのブランドの核になっている。

Brochure pages; 1993; CD, AD, D, CW: Terry Jones
P: Stefann Gentis / Thomas Kalak / Uli Wiesmeier DF: Start / Munich

73 Fire & Ice

Magazine ad; 1994; CD, AD, D: Terry Jones P: Stefan Ruiz DF: Start / Munich

"IT MAY SMELL LIKE SHIT TO YOU, BUT IT SMELLS LIKE MONEY

FEED YOUR MIND WITH THE LONGEST DAY OF YOUR LIFE

"is this bear on the way to shit'na...?"

Where the hell'd Chilkat?

Brochure; Autumn-Winter 1993-1994; CD, AD, D, CW: Terry Jones
P: Stefan Ruiz / Thomas Kalak DF: Start / Munich

Fire & Ice 75

towards the mountains

FIRE&ICE

Brochure; Spring-Summer 1994; CD, AD, D, CW: Terry Jones P: Stefan Ruiz CW: Kayt Jones DF: Start / Munich

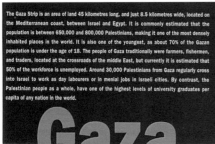

The Gaza Strip is an area of land 45 kilometres long, and just 8.5 kilometres wide, located on the Mediterranean coast, between Israel and Egypt. It is commonly estimated that the population is between 650,000 and 800,000 Palestinians, making it one of the most densely inhabited places in the world. It is also one of the youngest, as about 70% of the Gazan population is under the age of 18. The people of Gaza traditionally were farmers, fishermen, and traders, located at the crossroads of the middle East, but currently it is estimated that 50% of the workforce is unemployed. Around 30,000 Palestinians from Gaza regularly cross into Israel to work as day labourers or in menial jobs in Israeli cities. By contrast, the Palestinian people as a whole, have one of the highest levels of university graduates per capita of any nation in the world.

Gaza

ガザ地区とは、長さ45キロ、幅8.5キロにわたる、イスラエルとエジプトとの間の地中海に面した地域のことである。65万から80万のパレスチナ人が住んでいると推定され、世界中でも島も人口の密集した地域の一つである。若者の比率の最も多い場所の一つでもあり、人口の70%が18歳以下である。
ガザの人々はもともと中近東の国々との境界に暮らす農民や漁師や貿易商たちであった。現在は50%の就業年齢層の人々が失業中であると推定されている。およそ3万人のパレスチナ人が日雇い労働あるいは卑賤な仕事のために定期的にイスラエルの町へ渡っている。しかしそれとは対照的に、全体としてパレスチナ人は世界中のどの国よりも人口に対する大学卒業者の比率の高さを誇っている。

UNITED COLORS OF BENETTON.

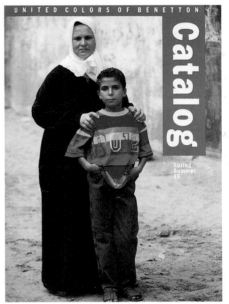

snacks 癖になっちゃうスナック

These are the world's snack foods, the things we eat because we love the way it feels when they crunch or squish between our teeth. これが世界のスナック。この食べ物がクセになっちゃうんだ。

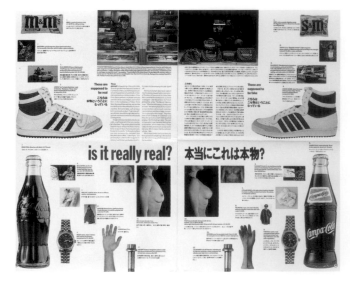

is it really real? 本当にこれは本物?

Hello, Lola? Have you heard? The world's super-powers can't fight anymore. Now they have to work together. But don't worry, competition isn't dead because...

ハロー、ローラ? もう聞いた? 世界の超大国はもう争うのをやめたんだって。これからは一緒にやっていかなきゃならないんだ。でも心配ないよ。競争なくなったわけじゃない。だって...

(Pretend this is a message from Pepsi and Coke.)

これはペプシとコカ・コーラからのメッセージということにしてみてね。

...the superproducts could stop spending money (and talent and resources) on ads that tell people about products and spend it on ads that tell people about the world...

スーパー・プロダクトはお金（才能や資源）を製品のことを人々に伝える広告のためより、世界のことを人々に伝える広告のために使うことができる

(Pretend this is a message from Sony and Philips.)

これはソニーとフィリップスからのメッセージということにしてみてね。

UNITED COLORS OF BENETTON.

clothed to naked

服を着てから裸になるまで

Adam and Eve were naked. It was fine. Then they ate an apple from Eden's Tree of Knowledge and it altered their world view. They became self-conscious. Naked was no longer fine. The lesson: How naked you think you are depends on where you get your apples.

United Colors of Benetton ✛ 85

PR magazine; Spring-Summer 1992; CD: Oliviero Toscani Editor: Tibor Kalman /
Karrie Jacobs / Lucy Schulte / Allce Albert / Alexis Jetter, others
D: Gary Koepke, others DF: Colors Editorial Offices

DIESEL
JEANS AND WORKWEAR

Top: Jib Pants: Fellow

Jacket: Slab Shorts: Maul

Diesel

Designer: Wilbert Das (Diesel Men) /
Marly Nijssen (Diesel Females) /
Peter Kimpkens (Diesel Kids) / Oliver Reboul (55DSL)
Country of original launch: Italy
Year of launch: 1978
Coverage: men's, women's, children's, casual apparel /
accessories / perfume

"We produce what we like. We do what we feel is right.
We are modern people in our global network and it seems,
what we like, a lot of people like too."

「自分たちがみずから好む物を創り出し、
正しい思うことを実行する ―― それが Diesel。
国境を越えて様々なつながりを持つ現代のなかで、
私たちが好む物は、多くの人々にも好まれるようだ」
(Johan Lindeberg / Marketing Director)

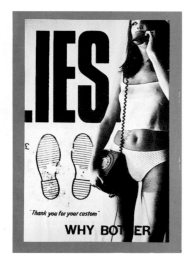

Magazine ad; 1994; BR: Diesel Shoes
CD, AD, D, CW: Brian Baderman
AD: Nick Oates / Dan Adams
P: Sandro Sodano
DF: Baderman (aka Unusual Enterprises)

Brochure page; Spring - Summer 1994;
CD, AD, D: Brian Baderman
AD, D, CW: Nick Oates AD, D: Dan Adams
P: Gautier Deblonde

Jeans label / tag; 1992-1994; D: Francesca Chiani / Josef Rossi

Package; 1992-1994; D: Francesca Chiani / Josef Rossi

Carrier bag; 1992-1994; D: Francesca Chiani / Josef Rossi

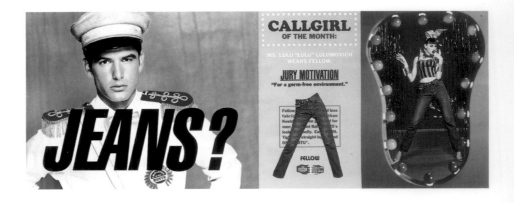

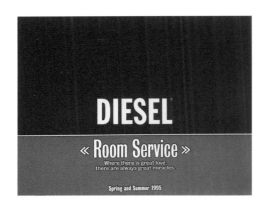

DIESEL

« Room Service »

Where there is great love,
there are always great miracles.

Spring and Summer 1995

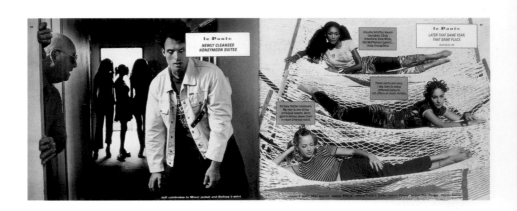

Brochure; Spring - Summer 1995; CD, AD, D, CW: Brian Baderman
AD, CW: Paradiset AD, D: Adam Whitaker D: Miles English
P: Henrik Halvarsson / Ellen von Unwerth DF: Baderman

89 Diesel

Poster; 1992-1994; D: Francesca Chiani / Josef Rossi

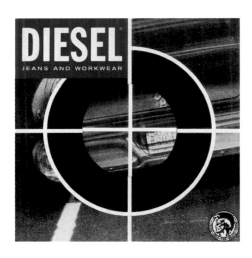

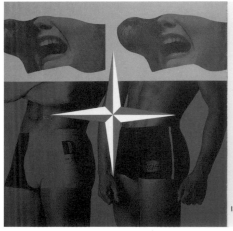

Brochure; Spring-Summer 1993; CD, AD, D, P, CW: Brian Baderman P: Nigel H. Case /
Fuel / Toby Glanville / Mike Smith / Andre Paradis DF: Baderman (aka Unusual Enterprises)

Brochure; Autumn-Winter 1992-1993; CD, AD, D, CW: Brian Baderman P: Cuenza / Negro /
Lucca / Gaddo / Ochiello / F. Gransden / Fuel DF: Baderman (aka Unusual Enterprises)

Watch Your Favourite Music 24-Hours a Day!

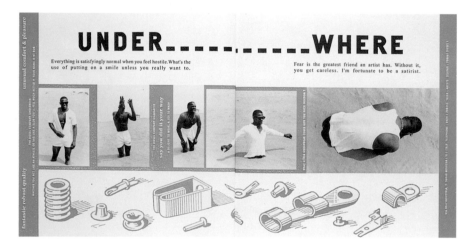

UNDER............WHERE

DIESEL
JEANS AND WORKWEAR

This publication may NOT be distributed to unlicensed personnel
THE ELEVENTH DIESEL CATALOG Autumn and Winter 1992-93

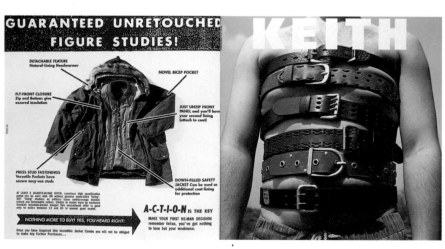

GUARANTEED UNRETOUCHED
FIGURE STUDIES!

KEITH

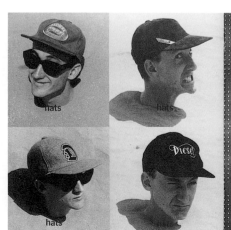

LIFTOFF

TURBO DIESEL FUEL

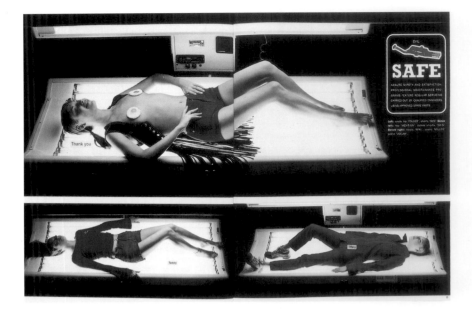

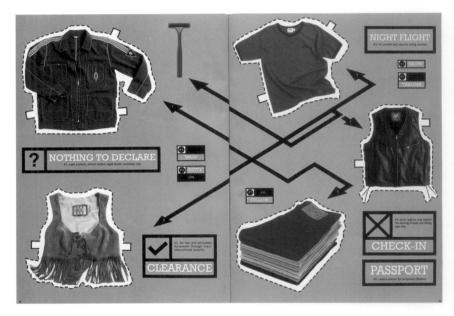

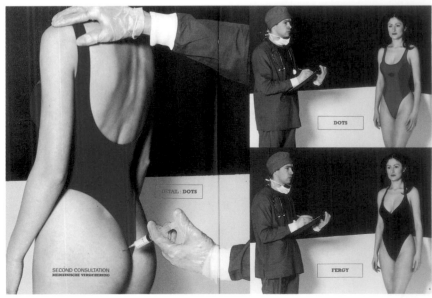

Spring-Summer 1994; CD, AD, D, P, CW: Brian Baderman AD, D: Adams
AD, D, P, CW: Nick Oates P: Sandro Sodano / Nigel Case / Jack Chessum / Donald Christie /
Glyn Howells / Gautier Deblonde I: Mike Croft / Nathan Ward DF: Baderman

Brochure; Autumn-Winter 1994-1995; CD, AD, D, P, CW: Brian Baderman
P: Sandro Sodano / Pierre Winther / Lloyd Ricketts CW: Whitaker / Philpot DF: Baderman

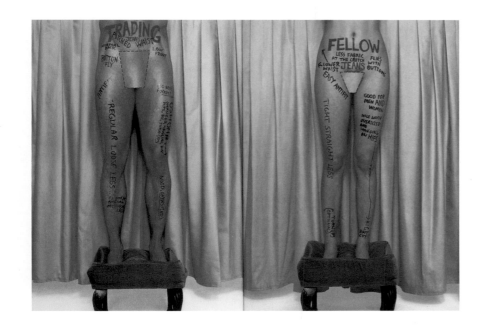

("cimarron")
blue jeans

Cimarron
TOTALMENTE FATAL

tag labels

Cimmarron

Country of original launch: France
Coverage: men's, women's,
children's, casual apparel

Jeans labels / tags

96 Cimarron

Cimarron ■ 97

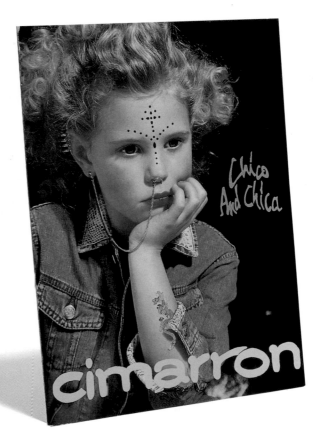

fRENCH CONNECTiON

Price tag; CD, AD, D: Valerie Wickes DF: Din Graphics

fRENCH CONNECTiON

French Connection

Country of original launch: England
Year of launch: 1972 (women's) / 1976 (men's) / 1986 (children's)
Coverage: men's, women's, children's apparel / accessories

For women, innovative design and quality fabrics for a definitive style. For men, individual style and high fashion that does not dictate. And fun-to-wear clothes for children in natural fibres.

完成されたスタイルを目指し、上質の素材を革新的なデザインに
仕立てたレディース。メンズはひかえめだが個性的なスタイルと
ハイ・ファッションを構築。そして子供向けには天然素材を
使った、着て楽しい服のデザインを提供している。

spring summer 94   FRENCH CONNECTION

Brochure; Spring-Summer 1994; CD, AD, D: Valerie Wickes P: Eamonn J. McCabe DF: Din Graphics

Leaflet; Autumn-Winter 1993; CD, AD, D: Valerie Wickes P: Julian Broad DF: Din Graphics

+ | 100 | French Connection

Leaflet; Spring-Summer 1994; CD, AD, D: Valerie Wickes P: Eamonn J. McCabe DF: Din Graphics

ESPRIT

Esprit

Country of original launch: USA
Year of launch: 1968
Coverage: women's, children's, casual apparel / accessories

The underlying concepts behind the Esprit World View are a clear understanding of target customers and a responsibility to the communities in which we operate.

客層の正確な把握と社会に対する責任の認識
──それがエスプリ・ワールドの根底になっている

REPLANT
reuse
rethink
reseed
replenish
reassess
reinform
renew
rechoose
100%
GROWTH
LIVE PRODUCT
ESPRIT

RESEED

GENUINE
Pure-Love
Forever Sincere
the secret
is to follow
your heart
ESPRIT

WEARING
ESPRIT
DENIM
quality
STYLISH FIT

ESPRIT
outd

POP display; 1993; D: Andrew Hoyne DF: Andrew Hoyne Design

Esprit 103 +

Leaflets; 1994; CD, D: Erin Lorch

T-shirt; 1994; CD, D, I: Erin Lorch

T-shirt; 1994; CD, D, I: Erin Lorch

+ 104 Esprit

T-shirt; 1994; CD, D, I: Erin Lorch

T-shirt; 1994; CD, D, I: Erin Lorch

Posters; 1993; AD, D: Andrew Hoyne
P: Rob Blackburn
DF: Andrew Hoyne Design

SISLEY

SISLEY

Country of original launch: Italy
Year of launch: 1975
Coverage: men's, women's, children's apparel /
accessories

Easy-to-wear elegance in outdoor styles on 'city' and
'countryside' themes. An attractively priced line-up for a
versatile wardrobe that adapts to formal occasions and
casual dressing.

都市と自然がテーマになり、アウトドア感覚ながら、
洗練された着こなしやすいアイテムを
打ち出している。また買いやすい価格帯も
魅力のひとつ。オン・オフタイムにも対応できる
ワードローブを揃えている。

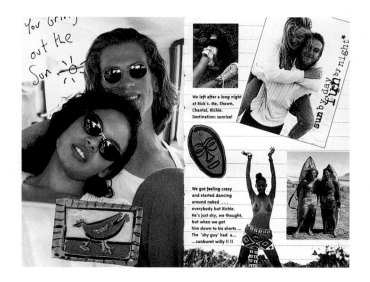

SISLEY + 107

Brochure; Spring-Summer 1994; CD: Nikko AD: Magnus Skogsberg P: Magnus Reed I: Lynne Douglas DF: Energy Project

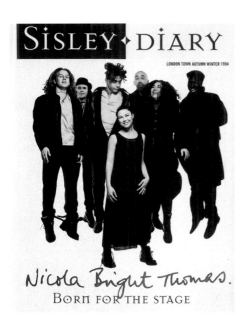

Brochure; Autumn-Winter 1994-1995; CD: Nikko AD: Maguns Skogsberg P: Magnus Reed DF: Energy Project

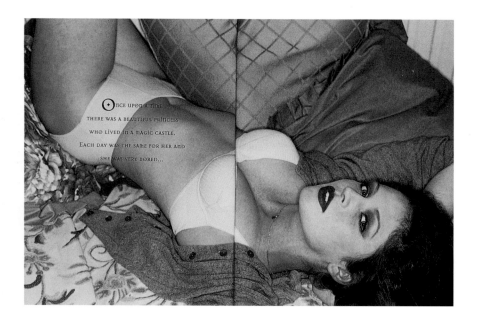

Once upon a time
there was a beautiful princess
who lived in a magic castle.
Each day was the same for her and
she was very bored...

horsing about. Time for some HORSEPLAY. Just rising about. Time for some HORSEPLAY. Just horsi

SISLEY · DIARY

LONDON TOWN AUTUMN WINTER 1994

Born for the stage
Nicola Bright Thomas

"Would madame, care for a cup of tea?"

Went down to Horley to see Cousin Joe (although she's not exactly my type!) Keith and Joe started messing about in the park like two overgrown kids. Barry the Butler pretended he was minding his own business but he was really spying on them. Joe and Keith got on like a house on fire and had a real laugh and a giggle. Then RED ALERT! My alarm bells start ringing. Time for me to step in...

Britain's foamiest
soap opera
"Girls in hot water"

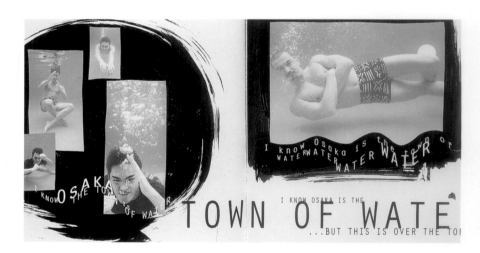

Brochure; Spring-Summer 1995; CD: Nikko P: Magnus Reed CW: Natalia Borri DF: Energy Project

Postcards; Spring-Summer 1995; CD: Nikko
P: Magnus Reed CW: Natalia Borri
DF: Energy Project

Corinne Cobson

Carrier bag / price tag

Corinne Cobson

Designer: Corinne Cobson
Country of original launch: France
Year of launch: 1986
Coverage: women's apparel

Straightforward design with a lively, punk flavor. No longer limited to apparel, the label now includes design for beach wear, tights and tableware.

シンプルなデザインの中に、パンキッシュでエネルギッシュな
雰囲気を持つブランド。洋服だけでなく、水着やタイツ、食器の
デザインも手がけている。

Direct mail material

Invitation card; Winter 1993-1994; P: Tanguy Loyzance

Invitation card; Summer 1994; P: Tanguy Loyzance

YOSHIKI HISHINUMA

YOSHIKI
HISHINUMA
1995 Spring & Summer
Collection
1994. 12. 2 (Fri)
Laforet Harajuku
Open 7:45pm · Start 8:15pm

Yoshiki Hishinuma

Designer: Yoshiki Hishinuma　菱沼良樹
Country of original launch: Japan
Year of launch: 1992
Coverage: women's apparel

A world-class designer with a strong artistic touch. His '95
spring / summer collection, 'Flowers and Plants', using tie-dyed
materials and chemically-treated velvets, won praise for its
innovative, provocative ideas.

デザインの中にアーティスティックな魅力を感じる
Yoshiki Hishinuma。'95年春夏コレクションでも「花と植物」
をテーマに、絞り加工や薬品で溶かしたベルベットを素材として使い、
その斬新で刺激的な発想が賞賛を得た。イタリア、ドイツ、
フランス等世界的レベルで活躍しているデザイナー。

p114 (top) Document folder D: Yoshiki Hishinuma / Bruno Munari

(bottom) Poster; Spring-Summer 1995; D: Takuya Onuki

Direct mail material; Autumn-Winter 1994-1995; D: Yoshiki Hishinuma

Direct mail material; Autumn-Winter 1992-1993; D: Yoshiki Hishinuma

Yoshiki Hishinuma 115

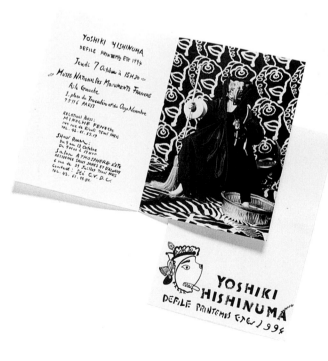

Direct mail material; Spring-Summer 1994; D: Yoshiki Hishinuma

Direct mail material; Autumn-Winter 1993-1994; D: Yoshiki Hishinuma

Tag / carrier bags; AD,D: Masuo Kuroda

I.S.

Designer: Sunao Kuwahara　桑原　直
Country of original launch: Japan
Year of launch: 1983
Coverage: women's apparel / accessories

A progressive range of everyday wear that matches the many
different requirements of the modern woman's lifestyle.

女性の生活を応援するために、色々な意味でバランスのとれた、
進行形の普段着を提案している。

I.S

Brochure; Spring-Summer 1995; AD,D: Masuo Kuroda P: Hibiki Kobayashi

GHOST

With Compliments

Ghost Limited   The Chapel   263 Kensal Road   London W10 5DB   Tel: 081 960 3121   Fax: 08...3374...

STYLE No:
DESCRIPTION:
FABRIC:
PRICE:
GHOST©

Ghost

Designer: Tanya Sarne
Country of original launch: England
Year of launch: 1984
Coverage: women's apparel

The name evokes ethereal, untouchable and illusive qualities. Ghost clothing can be described as simple, modern, realistic and functional.

不可思議で実際に触れることのできない、幻想的なイメージを
思い起こさせるブランド名とは対称的なGhostのファッション。
それはシンプル、モダン、現実的かつ機能的と言える。

1.

Ghost █ 119 ✚

2.

Ribbon / price tag / woben label D: Tanya Sarne / Angela South Well / Sophia Malig

GHOST

3.

1. Invitation card; Autumn-Winter 1994;
D: Tanya Sarne / Angela South Well /
Sophia Malig

2. Invitation card; Spring-Summer 1994;
D: Tanya Sarne / Angela South Well /
Sophia Malig

3. Invitation card; Autumn-Winter 1994;
D: Tanya Sarne / Angela South Well /
Sophia Malig

STUDIOV

Carrier bag; D: Natsuko Ono DF: Studio-V Design-Room

Gift towels; D: Natsuko Ono
DF: Studio-V Design-Room

Studio-V

Country of original launch: Japan
Year of launch: 1976
Coverage: women's apparel

A co-ordinates label that combines classic and modern values,
for smart, distinctive design and styling.

Classic & Modern（新旧の価値の融合）をコンセプトに、
小粋でクリアなデザインとスタイルを提案する
コーディネイト・ブランド。

Brochure; Spring-Summer 1989; AD: Susanne Bartsch P: Eisuke Ishimuro

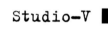

Studio-V ✚ 121

Direct mail material; Spring-Summer 1994;

DF: Studio-V Design-Room

nue au soleil
STUDIO V '01 SPRING-SUMMER

STUDIO V

Studio-V 123

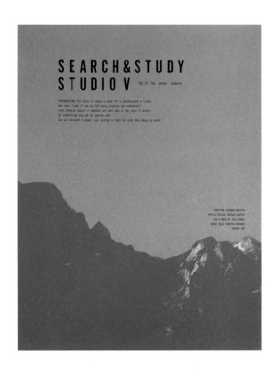

1.

2.

STUDIOV '93 FALL & WINTER COLLECTION

124 Studio-V

3.

4.

1990 FALL-WINTER COLLECTION
STUDIOV

drawing by RUBEN TOLEDO

5.

6.

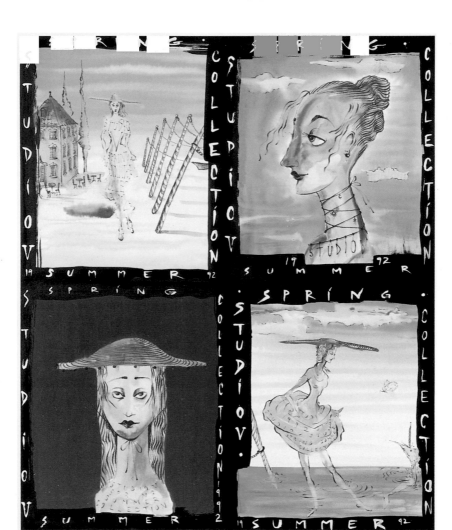

Poster; Spring-Summer 1992;
I: Ruben Toledo
DF: Studio-V Design-Room

Poster; Autumn-Winter 1992-1993;
I: Ruben Toledo
DF: Studio-V Design-Room

FIORUCCI

Logo; CD: Elio Fiorucci D: Architect Italo Luppi

Eighteen is the last one, a sweet honey-pie, shows off her bijoux to wish you

GOODBYE

Fiorucci

Designer: Elio Fiorucci
Country of original launch: Italy
Year of launch: 1967
Coverage: men's, women's, children's, casual apparel / accessories

Fiorucci's signature has remained "forever young" through the decades by playing with humour and opposites: being both sexy and tender, provoking or understated, romantic or trashy.

Fiorucciのテーマは **"forever young"**。そのテーマを何十年にも渡り、ユーモアあふれる遊び心と相反するイメージを組み合わせることによって守り続けている。セクシーで華奢、刺激的で控え目、ロマンチックでトラッシーと言う風に。

T-shirt gift pack / invitation card; Autumn-Winter 1995-1996; CD: Elio Fiorucci
AD: European Institute of Design Students

Magazine ad; 1994; CD: Elio Fiorucci AD, D: Fiorucci Team

Brochure; Spring-Summer 1995; CD: Elio Fiorucci AD: Corenzo de Grassi / Fiorucci Team P: Nick Ferrano

Nine are Twin Sisters from *Faraway North* Ice is a warm place rocking them both.

It's a lolly Seven fancies, Eight, hits you with dolly glances.

Fiorucci   129

abahouse ● devinette

Postcard / carrier bag; 1994-1995; I: Junko Sakuraba

SOLDES
abahouse ● devinette

SOLD
abahouse ● devin

130

abahouse · devinette

Designer: Yukio Otorii 大鳥居 幸男
Country of original launch: Japan
Year of launch: 1988
Coverage: women's apparel

For women who like to dress cool. French in flavour,
and never out-of-date, a style designed for women of
savvy and free-wheeling taste.

"Something cool、凛とした心意気を着るひとに ──"
がテーマ。フレンチ・テイストで、時代性という
フィルターを通しながら、いつも機知と不良ぼさを
失わない女性たちのためのスタイルを提案している。

Comme un miroir qui réfléchirait le temps.....

Postcard; 1993-1995; I: Junko Sakuraba

132 abahouse•devinette

Brochure / carrier bag; Spring - Summer 1995; AD: Masahiko Araki P: Mario Testino CW: Ikki Mori

Poster; Spring - Summer 1995; AD: Masahiko Araki P: Mario Testino CW: Ikki Mori

Defense de "re"

Remixer, recopier, readapter!
Pourquoi est-ce toujours
comme cela "re" ? Ne faudrait
pas bieutôt quelque chose de
totalement Nouveau?

Remixer, réabsorption, refrain,
réactivation, réadapter.
Réchauffage, recomposable,
reconnaître, recopier,
recorriger, recoudre, réemploi.
Recréation, récreation?
Réclame, recommenceur, recoupe,
rediseur, refaiseur, remanieur,
resigner, reptile, reclus, réchappe?
Pourquoi est-ce toujours
comme cela "re"?
Ne faudrait pas bieutôt
quelque chose de
totalement Nouveau?
Photographed by Mario Testino

abahouse devinette

+ 134 abahouse•devinette

abahouse devinette
COLLECTION AUTOMNE·HIVER '93/'94

abahouse•devinette ✚ 135

Postcard; Autumn-Winter 1992-1993; AD: Masahiko Araki
D: Kie Wakamatsu P: Tiziano Magni I: Junko Sakuraba

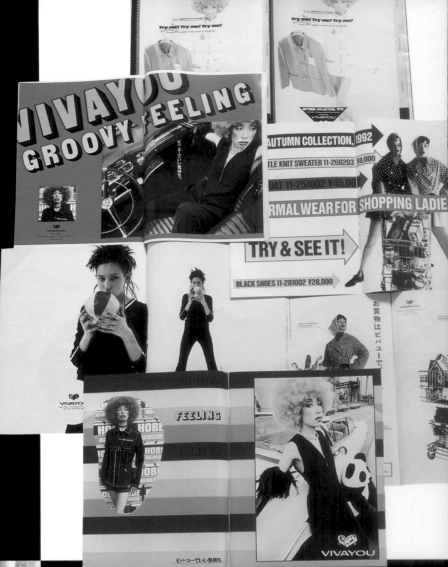

VIVAYOU

Designer: Shiori Egi　江木 志保利
Country of original launch: Japan
Year of launch: 1977
Coverage: women's apparel

Toasting the new generation of active young women. A look to
delight today's lively young girls characterized by chic city clothes
that help to put over an individual fashion statement.

"VIVA"=「万歳」と**"YOU"**=「パワフルな女の子」を意味する
ブランド名そのままに、現代の、健康的でキュートな
女の子たちをとりこにしているファッション。
彼女たちの自己主張を手助けする、小粋で都会的な服作りが特徴。

VIVAYOU 137

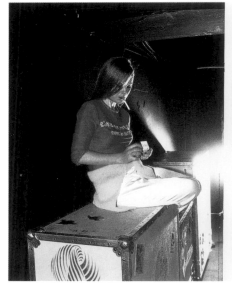

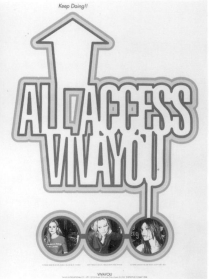

Brochure; Spring 1995; CD: Hiroko Kawasaki Editorial Director: Fumihiro Hayashi AD, D: Yuichi Miyashi P: Sofia Coppola DF: Tycoon Graphics

Brochure; Autumn 1994; AD, D: Yuichi Miyashi P: Kazunari Tajima / Tsutomu Tanaka CW: Ayumi Kawasaki DF: Tycoon Graphics

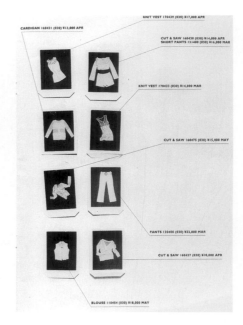

Brochure; Summer 1994; AD, D: Yuichi Miyashi P: Kazunari Tajima DF: Tycoon Graphics

IN A SUNNY
PLACE.........
VIVA YOU
WINTER
COLLECTION
1993
OPEN
UP!! YOU'LL BE A
DREAMER. ENJOY
YOUR LIFE!!

VIVAYOU 141

vivayou spring 1994

The Ozone Community

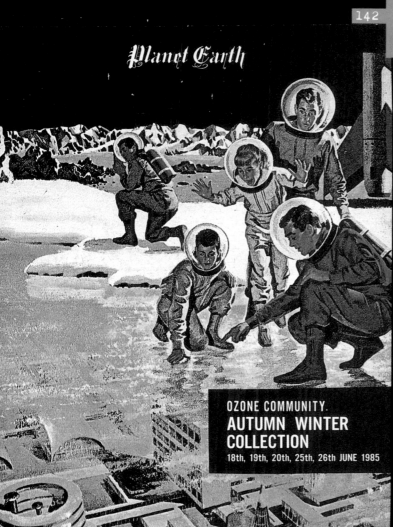

Planet Earth

**OZONE COMMUNITY.
AUTUMN WINTER
COLLECTION**
18th, 19th, 20th, 25th, 26th JUNE 1985

Ozone Community

Designer: Katsuzou Yamaguchi　山口勝三
Country of original launch: Japan
Year of launch: 1978
Coverage: women's, casual apparel / accessories

Using mostly natural fibres, we create clothes with a sense of
the unique dynamism of the times, hand craffed, and with an
appealing originality.

天然素材を中心に、時代の中に独特のムーブメントを感じる
服を作り続けている。またハンドメイドを基本に考え、
オリジナル・メッセージをアピールしている。

HYSTERIC GLAMOUR
TOKYO LONDON

Hysteric Glamour

Designer: Nobuhiko Kitamura　北村信彦
Country of original launch: Japan
Year of launch: 1984
Coverage: men's, women's, casual apparel /
accessories

Evoking the 60's and 70's subculture (rock'n'roll,
surfing, car-junkies) through a unique and highly
individual style, this label is centred on enduring and
ever-popular street fashion.

60's～70'sに見られるサブカルチャー（ロック、
サーファー、カージャンキー）等を、
個性的な独自のスタイルで表現。
トレンドで終わらない、根付いた
ストリート・ファッションを展開している。
。

FOR YANKEE GIRL
THE KIDS ARE ALRIGHT
DIZZY & MILKY
HYSTERI
AND THE
"GLAMOUR"
ALL TICKET SOLD

Package / Carrier bags; CD, AD, D: Nobuhiko Kitamura
p145 Stickers / woven labels; 1990-1993; AD: Nobuhiko Kitamura

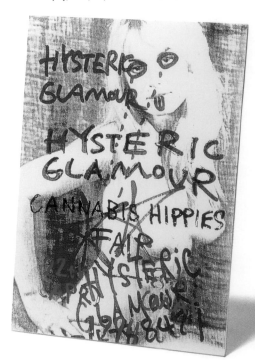

Poster; 1992; AD, D, I: Nobuhiko Kitamura

146 Hysteric Glamour

POP display; 1993; CD: Michael Koppelmen D: Nobuhiko Kitamura

POP display; 1994; AD, D, P: Nobuhiko Kitamura

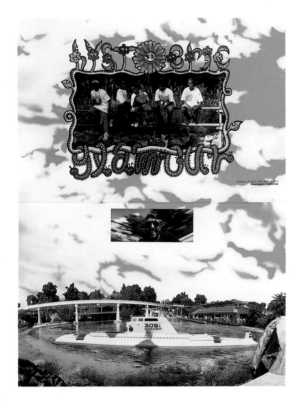

Brochure; AD: Osamu Wataya D: Miyuki Kamiya P: Kiyoshi Tatsukawa I: Stephen Bliss Coordinator: Hinako Hoshi Editor: Takarajima Magazine

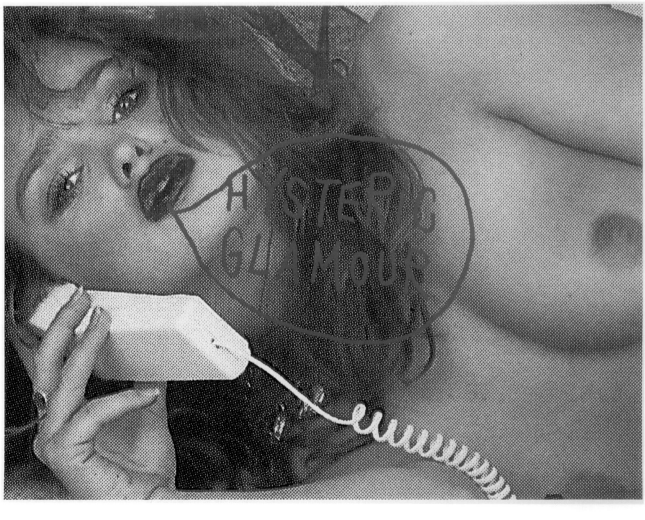

Posters; 1995; AD: Nobuhiko Kitamura

Brochure; 1994; AD: Nobuhiko Kitamura D: Osamu Wataya

150 Hysteric Glamour

T-shirt; 1995; D: Nobuhiko Kitamura

T-shirt; 1995; D: Nobuhiko Kitamura

Hysteric Glamour 151

T-shirt; 1995; D: Nobuhiko Kitamura

Accessories

Red or Dead

Designer: Wayne Hemingway
Country of original launch: England
Year of launch: 1983
Coverage: men's, women's apparel / accessories

Red or Dead's main aim is to produce innovative, challenging
fashion at affordable prices and on a non-elitist level.

斬新で挑戦的なファッションを常に作り出している
Red or Dead。また一般の人々向けに、手ごろな価格で
提供もしている。

Red or Dead ■ 155

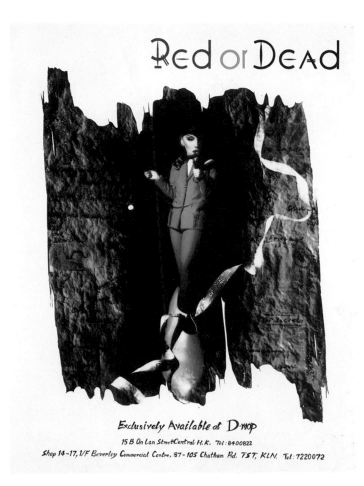

Red or Dead

Exclusively Available at D·mop

15 B On Lan Street Central H.K.   Tel : 8400822

Shop 14–17, 1/F Beverley Commercial Centre, 87–105 Chatham Rd. TST, KLN.   Tel : 7220072

Magazine ad; 1992; CD: Sue Fok DF: D-MOP

for
spring
and
summer
1994

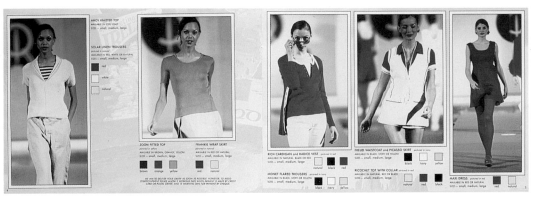

Brochure; Spring-Summer 1994; CD: Gary Page (front cover) P: Andrew Thomas / Martin Ridgewell DF: Red or Dead

Direct mail material; Autumn-Winter 1994-1995; CD: Gary Page AD: Joachim Sedelmeier D: Keith Stevenson DF: Red or Dead

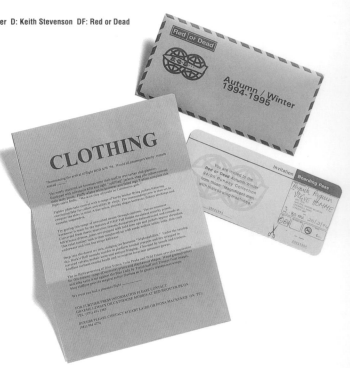

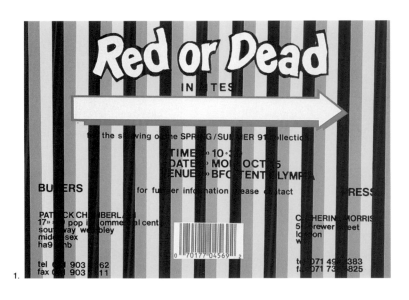

1.

2.

3.

1. Invitation card; Spring-Summer 1991; CD: Wayne Hemingway
   D: Kate Cullinan / Gary Page DF: Red or Dead

2. Invitation card; Autumn-Winter 1991-1992; CD: Catherine Morris
   DF: Red or Dead

3. Invitation card; Spring-Summer 1992; D: Kate Cullinan DF: Red or Dead

Brochure; Spring-Summer 1993; AD: Kath Derlin P: Suresh Karadia / Paul Westbrooke DF: Red or Dead

Red or Dead   157

PR Magazine; Autumn-Winter 1989; CD: Catherine Morris D: Geoffrey Stephenson I: Chris Long DF: Red or Dead

Brochure; 1991; AD, D: David Nethercott / Sophia M. Tampakopoulos P: Neil Robinson DF: Red or Dead

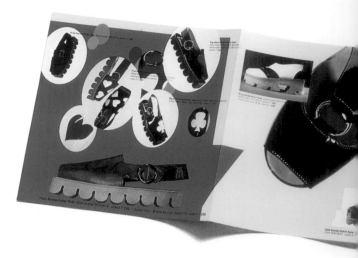

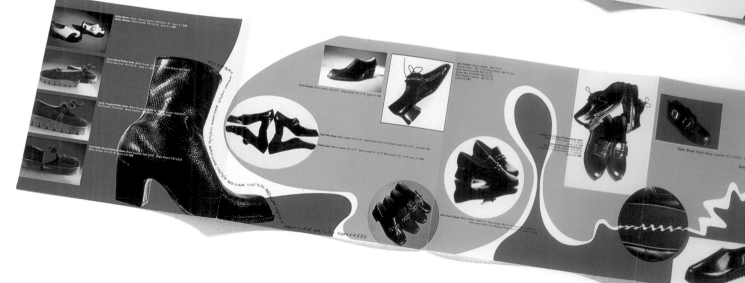

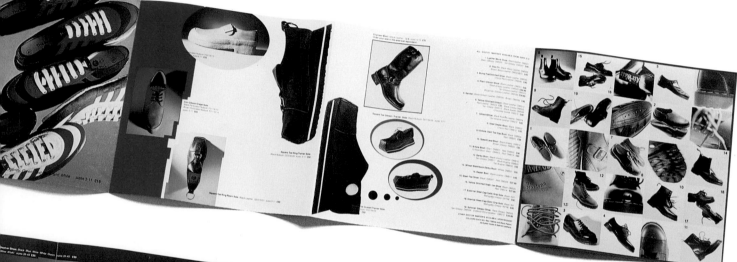

Brochure; 1990; DF: A Gas Design

4°C

(top) Brochure; 1994; AD: Miyuki Hirashima P: Takao Shioguchi

(bottom) POP display; 1995; AD: Miyuki Hirashima P: Meisa Fujishiro

995 Men's Goods
Collection

4°C

4 °C

Country of original launch: Japan
Year of launch: 1968
Coverage: women's apparel / accessories / perfume

With a philosophy of exploring unique concepts rather than following
established trends, this accessories brand has carved a niche
through researching new fields without relying on particular
materials or items.

流行を追うのではなく、あくまでも独自のコンセプトに基づいた
もの作りを基本スタイルにしている。素材やアイテムに
こだわらない、常に新しい分野での商品開発によって、業界でも
ひとつの位置を築いている。

Carrier bags; AD: 4°C advertising sales promotion section

Packages; AD: 4°C advertising sales promotion section

Gift towel / soap / self-adhesive notes; 1994-1995; AD: 4°C advertising sales promotion section

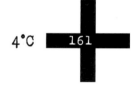

4°C 161

Brochure; 1995; AD: Miyuki Hirashima P: Meisa Fujishiro

Brochure; 1994; AD: Nimiko Mizutani

Brochure; 1994; AD: Nimiko Mizutani

162 4°C

Postcards; Summer 1992, 1994; AD: Miyuki Hirashima P: Tadayuki Naito / Masao Ota

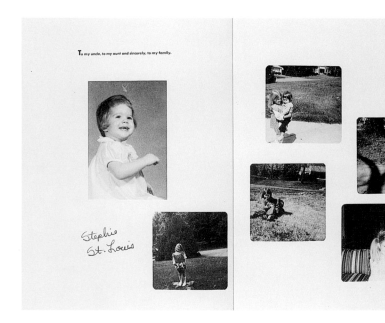

To my uncle, to my aunt and sincerely, to my family.

Stephie
St. Louis

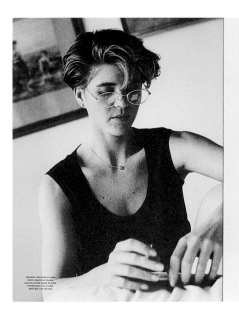

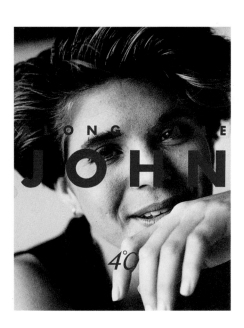

ONCE MORE
JOHN
4°C

John and I took a train. We got to the town by the beach. There was high voice and high roar coming out of the wave. I couldn't even hear it, but it made John think.

Brochure; Summer 1992; AD: Miyuki Hirashima P: Yoshi Ohara

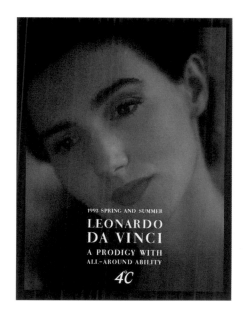

1993 SPRING AND SUMMER
LEONARDO DA VINCI
A PRODIGY WITH ALL-AROUND ABILITY
4°C

Brochure; Spring-Summer 1993; AD: Miyuki Hirashima P: Ryoichi Saito

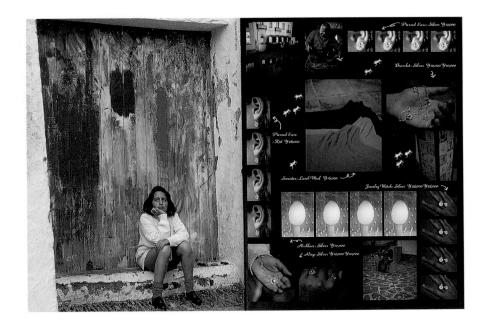

agete

agete

6-7-4 Minami-Aoyama Minato-ku Tokyo Japan 107 Telephone 03-3400-2202

agete

Country of original launch: Japan
Year of launch: 1990
Coverage: accessories

A jewellery collection that is simple and elegant in design,
and well-tuned to the times.

シンプルで洗練されたデザインの中にも、
時代感覚のあるジュエリーを集めたブランド

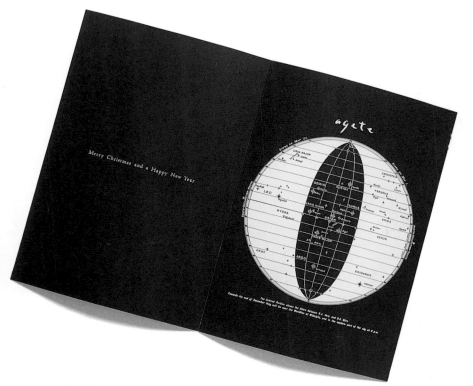

Carrier bag / Packages; CD: Yukiko Maekawa
AD: Sazaby Graphic Design D: Reiko Nogami

Greeting card; 1991-1992; CD: Yukiko Maekawa AD: Sazaby Graphic Design
D: Hatsuko Kobayashi / Hitoshi Maeda

agete 167

1.

1. Postcard; 1991; CD: Yukiko Maekawa
   AD: Sazaby Graphic Design
   D: Hatsuko Kobayashi

2. Postcard; Spring-Summer 1992;
   CD: Yukiko Maekawa
   AD: Sazaby Graphic Design
   D: Hatsuko Kobayashi / Yukiko Yamazaki

3. Postcard; 1990; CD: Yukiko Maekawa
   AD: Sazaby Graphic Design D: Reiko Nogami

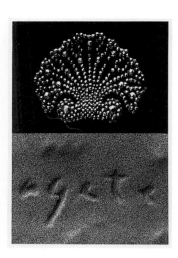

2.

3.

p166 (bottom) Carrier bag / packages; CD: Yukiko Maekawa AD: Sazaby Graphic Design
D: Reiko Nogami / Hatsuko Kobayashi / Chisako Nishimura

Greeting cards / tag label; 1992-1994; CD: Yukiko Maekawa AD: Sazaby Graphic Design
D: Hatsuko Kobayashi / Yukiko Yamazaki P: Toshiro Takayama

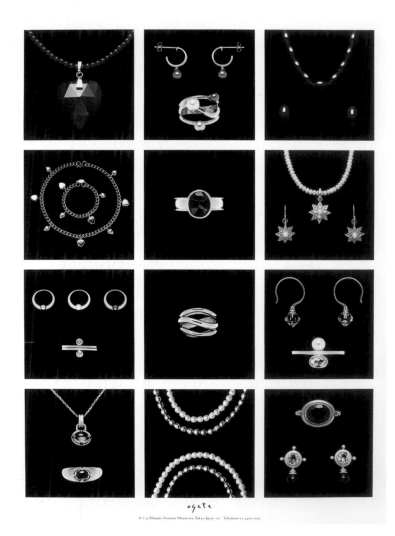

agete

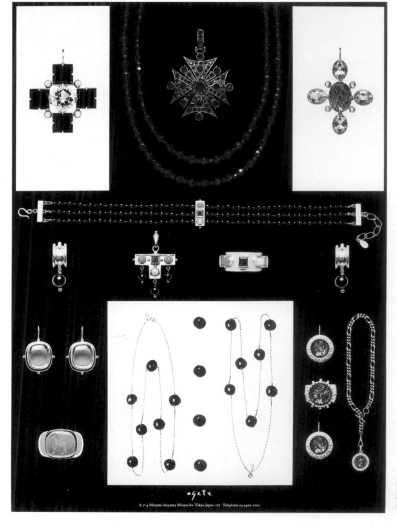

Direct mail materials; 1994; CD: Yukiko Maekawa
AD: Sazaby Graphic Design D: Hatsuko Kobayashi /
Yukiko Yamazaki P: Takashi Mizushima

Cosmetics

Carrier bag; CD, AD, D: Kenji Ohishi
DF: C. S. F. Wood

METABOLIZING SKIN CARE
EFFECTOR COOL PRESERVE

METABOLIZING SKIN CARE
ESSENCE FOR PORE

METABOLIZING SKIN CARE
ESSENCE WHITENING EV

Leaflets; 1993-1994; CD, AD: Kenji Ohishi D: Miwa Ono P: Yukio Shimizu CW: Yoko Tada DF: C. S. F. Wood

ひとりひとりが例外です。コスメチック イプサ

Ipsa

Country of original launch: Japan
Year of launch: 1986
Coverage: cosmetics

Ipsa means 'cosmetics to suit the individual'. The customer and Ipsa
beautician together draw on data and technical resources to create
an individual 'formula' for the perfect choice of cosmetics.

「個に対応する化粧品」、それがイプサ。最も自分に相応しい化粧品
とするために、自分に合った使いこなしの「レシピ」を、情報と
技術で、お客様とスタッフが一緒に創造することを提唱している。

Direct mail material; 1993-1994; CD: Kenji Ohishi AD: Yasushi Nakamura D: Takashi Ito P: Shinichi Kaneko CW: Keiko Ehara DF: C. S. F. Wood

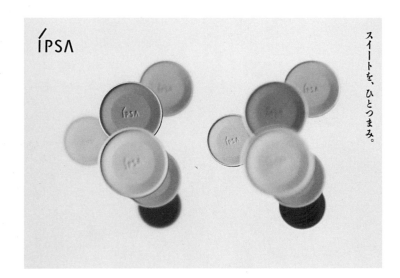

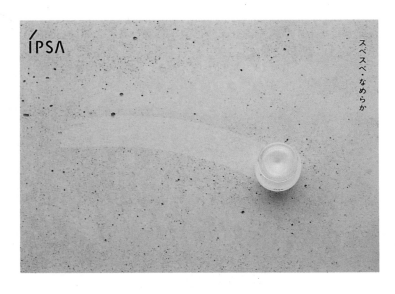

p170 (bottom) Poster; CD: Hiroshi Tanaka AD, D: Toshio Yamagata P: Francis Giacobetti CW: Naoko Serikawa DF: C. S. F. Wood

MY OWN

AT IPSA THERE IS NO

METHOD. THE AIM I

THEIR OWN, PERSON

AND IT IS ONE'S REC

A RECIPE BRINGS TO

INFORMATION, AND

COMBINED AND IN W

IT IS ONE OF THE KE

ONE'S BEAUTY IN O

IPSA TAKES GREAT

WITH YOU YOUR VE

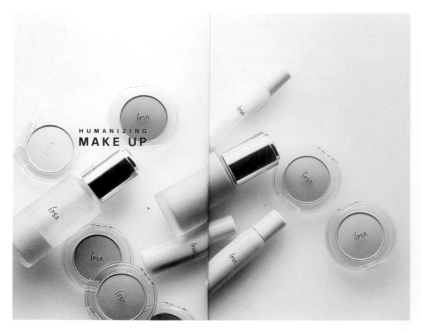

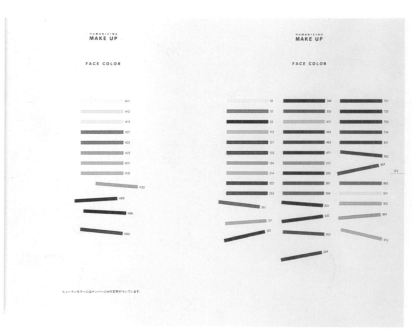

Brochure; 1994; CD, AD: Kenji Ohishi D: Yasushi Nakamura P: Francis Giacobetti / Yukio Shimizu CW: Yoshinobu Tamura / Rie Hirosawa DF: C. S. F. Wood

Magazine ad; 1994; CD, AD: Kenji Ohishi D: Yasushi Nakamura P: Yukio Shimizu CW: Yoko Tada DF: C. S. F. Wood

Magazine ad; 1994; CD, AD: Kenji Ohishi D: Miwa Ono P: Francis Giacobetti CW: Yoshinobu Tamura DF: C. S. F. Wood

174 Ipsa

Handout card; 1993; CD, AD: Kenji Ohishi D: Miwa Ono P: Toshiro Yamaguchi CW: Yoko Tada DF: C. S. F. Wood

Invitation card; 1994; CD, AD: Kenji Ohishi D: Reiko Harajo DF: C. S. F. Wood

Handout card; 1993; CD, AD: Kenji Ohishi D: Miwa Ono P: Toshiro Yamaguchi CW: Yoko Tada DF: C. S. F. Wood

Member's card; CD: Hiroshi Tanaka
AD: Toshio Yamagata D: Yuiro Nakamura
DF: C. S. F. Wood

Leaflet; 1994; CD, AD: Kenji Ohishi D: Miwa Ono P: Yukio Shimizu CW: Yoko Tada DF: C. S. F. Wood

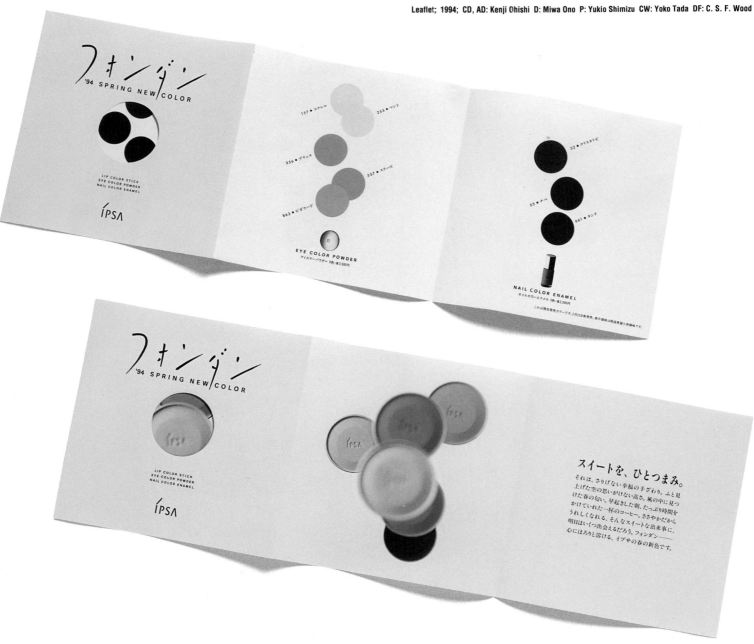

Leaflet; 1994; CD, AD: Kenji Ohishi D: Miwa Ono P: Toshiro Yamaguchi CW: Yoko Tada DF: C. S. F. Wood

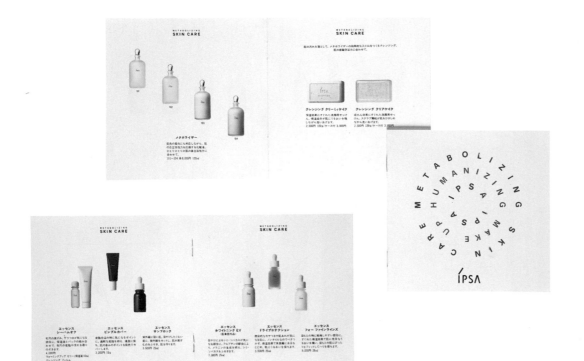

N° 105

N° 104

N° 103

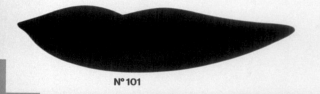

N° 102

N° 101

Kesalan Patharan

Designer: Saburo Watanabe　渡辺サブロオ
Country of original launch: Japan
Year of launch: 1988
Coverage: cosmetics / perfume

A brand of cosmetics produced to professional specifications,
developed by the hair and make-up designer Saburo Watanabe.
Easy to use, in definitive colours, these cosmetics exemplify quality.

ケサラン パサランはヘアメイク・デザイナー「渡辺サブロオ」
のプロデュースのもと、プロユース仕様のコスメティック・
ブランドとして開発・製品化された。使い易く発色が良い ──
品質を追求したこだわりの化粧品。

+ 178 Kesalan Patharan

Magazine ads; 1993-1994; AD: Koji Mizutani D: Hiroshi Ohmizo P: Minsei Tominaga DF: Mizutani Studio

Leaflet; 1991; AD: Koji Mizutani DF: Mizutani Studio

ケサランパサランのスキンケアは、メイクアップを美しく仕上げるための
シンプルな3ステップのシステムです。

スプリングミスト ミネラルウォーターアトマイザー

1. CLEANSING

クレンジングローション

2. TONING

スキントニック

3. MOISTURISING

モイストライジングローション

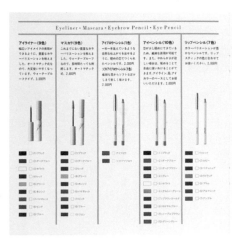

Eyeliner・Mascara・Eyebrow Pencil・Eye Pencil

アイライナー(9色) マスカラ(9色) アイブロウペンシル アイペンシル(10色) リップペンシル(7色)

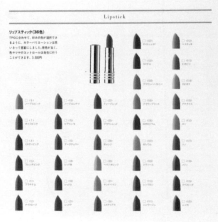

Lipstick

リップスティック(36色)

Kesalan Patharan ✚ 179

素肌のストレスレスを基本コンセプトに、
化粧する肌のためのスキンケアとして開発されました。

Kesalan Patharan

バトンタッチプログラムの提案

化粧品における過剰で余分な配合が適切なスキンケアを妨げています。
大切なのは、一つ一つのアイテムがそれぞれの段階的な役割をしっかり果た
し、次のプロセスへ効果的につないでいくことです。
そんな考え方から生まれたケサランパサランのスキンケアシリーズは、
アイテムごとの有効成分がその目的に応じて、必要な分をしっかりにしぼり
こまれています。
そして、その効果を最大に引き出すのがバトンタッチプログラム。
スキンケアからメイクアップまでを、クレンジングートーニング(モイスチュ
アコントロール)ーモイストライジング(エモリエントコントロール)ートリート
メントープロテクションの5つのステップに分け、組合せでつないでいく、
シンプルで確実な方法です。
バトンタッチプログラムは、ケサランパサランが提案する新しいスキン
ケアシステムです。

リメイクの提案 美しい肌をいつまでも保ち、そして続けるためにおすすめします。

「素肌のストレスレス」には朝・昼・夜の時間に応じたスキンケアが大切です。

Morning Care 朝、日覚めの肌は、眠っている間の皮脂や汗、ホコリなどで意外に汚れているもの。
水だけでの洗顔では、肌の透明感は得られません。
キメの細かい泡の洗顔フォームで肌をしっかり洗浄することがモーニングケアの基本。
バトンタッチプログラムの5つのステップで、外気の刺激や紫外線から肌を守りながら、
美しいメイクアップで一日のスタートを。

Day Care 昼、肌のストレスは受けています。

Night Care 夜、皮膚細胞が活発に働きだす時間。

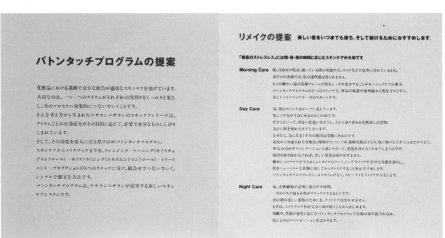

Leaflet; 1993; AD: Koji Mizutani D: Hiroshi Ohmizo DF: Mizutani Studio

shu uemura
tokyo paris new york

Shu Uemura

Designer: Shu Uemura / Daisuke Nakatsuka
植村　秀／中塚大輔
Country of original launch: Japan
Year of launch: 1965
Coverage: cosmetics / perfume

"Chanel linked cosmetics to fashion,
but Shu Uemura linked cosmetics to art."
From his own aesthetic ideals he has created cosmetics that
combine science with an artistic sensitivity.

「シャネルは化粧品をファッションと結びつけたが、
シュウ ウエムラは化粧品を芸術と結びつけた」といわれる
シュウ ウエムラ化粧品
独自の美容理論の元、科学と芸術的感性を
結びつけた化粧品を開発している

Boutique; AD: Daisuke Nakatsuka DF: Nakatsuka Daisuke Inc.

顔が主張しすぎると、あなたが見えなくなります. シュウ ウエムラ

+ 181 Shu Uemura

Boutique; AD: Daisuke Nakatsuka DF: Nakatsuka Daisuke Inc.

これからは、60歳代の美人が、ふえるでしょう. シュウ ウエムラ

Poster; 1993; AD, CW: Daisuke Nakatsuka D: Masami Ishibashi
P: Shozo Nakamura CW: Masakazu Nifuji DF: Nakatsuka Daisuke Inc.

プロの道具やテクニックを公開します。

シュウ ウエムラのブティックには、よそにはないメイクアップ製品やいろいろな道具が
ある。こんな評判は、決しておおげさではありません。日本を代表するメイクアップアー
ティスト、シュウ ウエムラは、画家が自分の道具を自作するように、自分のために化粧
品をつくるところから始めました。ここにご紹介するハード フォーミュラは、その一例。
美しい眉を描くために計算された、ほどよい堅さを保持。さらに写真のようになきかた状
に削ることによって、自然な眉が1本1本きれいに描けるのです。シュウ ウエムラは言
います。「初めてハリウッド映画のアシスタントについた時は、3日間、鉛筆削りばかりや
らされていた」と。ブティックにはプロの仕事場から生まれた知恵が、数多く存在します。

私の化粧箱からはじまりました。シュウ ウエムラ

洗顔オイルのシュウ ウエムラと呼ばれて、

もうだいぶ長い年月がたちます。その歴史を振りかえると、1850年代までさかのぼります。
ハリウッドでメイクアップを手がけていたシュウ ウエムラは、ある日、1本のビンを発
見します。それが、写真の"アンマスク"当時この洗顔オイルをエリザベス・テーラー、ル
シル・ボール、サンドラ・ディーなどとの女優たちがひそかに愛用していました。きびしい
環境のなかで1日に何度もメイクをつくっては落とす彼女たちは、オイルの高級を知っ
ていたのです。「オイルの生みの親、J・ウォーマックがこれもらっていけ、と言ってくれた」
と、シュウ ウエムラは、当時をなつかしみます。それ以降流れた長い時間は、彼がこの
オイルを根本から改良して、完成品とし、世界へと遊輸出していった歴史と、重なります。

信頼性がなければ、化粧品といえない。

もし子供が誤って口に入れたとしても、安全な化粧品でありたい。シュウ ウエムラの化
粧品の信頼性にかける意気込みには大きなものがあります。彼の母上が、肌の弱い人だっ
たこともあって、無着色、無香料は、自然成分の活用とともに、創業以来のメインテーマ
になっています。シュウ ウエムラ スキンケアは、そうした彼の到達点。彼は、その美
容理論"ビューティ リサイクル"(1980)のなかで次のように述べています。「過度の生理
作用にかかった正しい化粧品を使って、正しい化粧をつけると、肌のよい新陳代謝が促
進され、肌は次第次第によくなっていく」と。シュウ ウエムラの考え方は、いつも時代に
さきがけ、物事の本質をついています。次はどんなスキンケアをおととけできるでしょう。

Brochure; 1994; AD, CW: Daisuke Nakatsuka D: Kanna Numajiri P: Shozo Nakamura DF: Nakatsuka Daisuke Inc.

Brochure; 1993; AD: Daisuke Nakatsuka D: Masami Ishibashi P: Shozo Nakamura CW: Masakazu Nifuji DF: Nakatsuka Daisuke Inc.

ブティックは、顔をつくるアトリエである。

ブティックの発想は、開かれたアトリエです。かつてシュウ ウエムラの仕事場には、た
くさんのモデルたちが集まりました。彼女たちは、鏡のまえの化粧品をどんなによろこび
長い時間をかけてあそんでいたことか。みて、さわって、自由に楽しむ。彼は、このよろ
こびをすべての女性に捧げたいと考えました。実際、シュウ ウエムラのブティックには
大きなテスター台が置かれています。このシステムをとりいれたのは、彼のお店がはじめ
て。鏡をみながら、あらゆる化粧品を試用でき、じぶんの肌や顔にいちばん合ったものが
選べるようになったのです。そこには、誰もあなたに干渉する人はいません。「何時間で
も好きなだけ、私のアトリエで遊んでいってください」と、シュウ ウエムラは語ります。

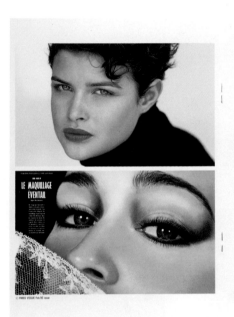

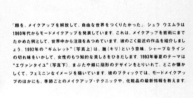

最新のメイクアップを教えます。

「顔を、メイクアップを解放して、自由な世界をつくりたかった」シュウ ウエムラは
1960年代からモードメイクアップを発表しています。これは、メイクアップを芸術にまで
たかめた例として、世界中から注目をあつめています。彼のごく最近の作品を紹介しまし
ょう。1992年の"ギムレット"(写真上)は、錐(キリ)という意味。シャープなライン
の切れ味をいかして、女性のもつ知的な美しさをひきだします。1993年春夏のテーマは
"エヴァンタイユ"(写真下)まぶたや頬に扇形の陰影のデザインをとりいれて、どこか悩か
しくて、フェミニンをイメージを描いています。彼のブティックでは、モードメイクアッ
プのほかにも、季節ごとのメイクアップ・テクニックや、化粧品の最新情報を教えます。

私のアトリエに遊びにきませんか。
シュウ ウエムラ

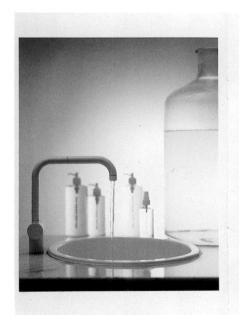

シュウ ウエムラの、洗顔オイルという神話。

1960年代、シュウ ウエムラがハリウッドでメイクアップを手がけていた頃、マジックオ
イルと呼ばれる洗顔オイルに出会いました。当時、この化粧品をひそかに愛用していたの
が、エリザベス・テーラー、サンドラ・ディー、パティ・ペイジなどのスターたち。彼は
やがて帰国後、みずから洗顔オイルの研究をはじめ、その改良にみごとに成功しました。以
来、簡単に使えて、ふかい汚れまでとりさる洗顔オイルは、シュウ ウエムラの代表作と
して、女性たちの支持を得ています。彼によると、スキンケアには次のような大切なポイントが
あります。「余分なものを与えすぎず、肌が本来もっている力をひきだすこと」。シュウ
ウエムラは、洗顔オイルにはじまる、シンプルな3ステップ・スキンケアを提唱します。

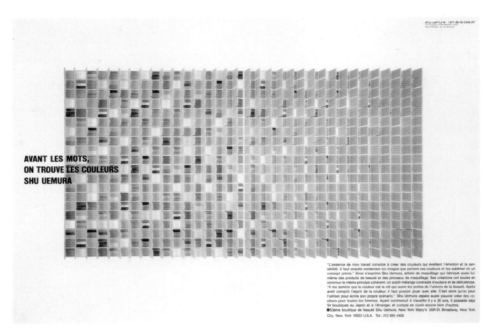

AVANT LES MOTS,
ON TROUVE LES COULEURS
SHU UEMURA

Magazine ad; 1987; AD, CW: Daisuke Nakatsuka D: Masato Isobe / Yuko Suzuki P: Shozo Nakamura DF: Nakatsuka Daisuke Inc.

Poster; 1990; AD, CW: Daisuke Nakatsuka D: Sonomi Sato P: Shozo Nakamura DF: Nakatsuka Daisuke Inc.

Poster; 1990; AD, CW: Daisuke Nakatsuka D: Sonomi Sato P: Yoichi Nagata DF: Nakatsuka Daisuke Inc.

メイクは、生涯学習です。

Magazine ad; 1988; AD, CW: Daisuke Nakatsuka D: Sonomi Sato
P: Sakae Tamura , Masataka Takayama CW: Hideo Okano DF: Nakatsuka Daisuke Inc.

顔は、生きている。

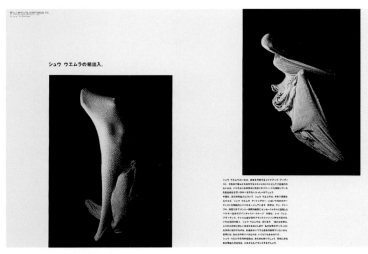

シュウ ウエムラの輸出入。

Shu Uemura ＋ 185

LES ÉCHANGES CULTURELS
DE SHU UEMURA

Magazine ad; 1987; AD, CW: Daisuke Nakatsuka D: Masato Isobe /
Yuko Suzuki / Sonomi Sato P: Yoichi Nagata DF: Nakatsuka Daisuke Inc.

ELIZABETH ARDEN

The fragrance dreams are made of

WHITE DIAMONDS

ELIZABETH TAYLOR

Elizabeth Arden

Country of original launch: USA
Year of launch: 1910
Coverage: cosmetics / perfume

Fragrances are associated with a specific mood or image: romantic, sensuous, bright, ethereal… Skincare products feature a technologically advanced formulation.

ロマンチック、審美的、聡明、不可思議 ── そんなムードや イメージを連想させるフレグランス。一方、スキンケア商品は 最先端の技術に基づいて作られている。

Magazine ad; 1991; CD: Paulette Dufault AD: Ranee Flynn P: Bruce Weber CW: Suzanne Hooper DF: Elizabeth Arden

1. Magazine ad; 1993; CD: Paulette Dufault AD: Ranee Flynn P: Patrick Demarchelier CW: Suzanne Hooper DF: Elizabeth Arden

2. Magazine ad; 1994; CD: Paulette Dufault AD: Ranee Flynn P: Robert Tardio CW: Suzanne Hooper DF: Elizabeth Arden

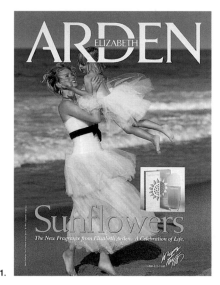

1.

2.

Elizabeth Arden ▉ 187

3.

4.

3. Magazine ad; 1992; CD: Paulette Dufault AD: Ranee Flynn P: Sante D'Orazio CW: Suzanne Hooper DF: Elizabeth Arden

4. Magazine ad; 1994; CD: Paulette Dufault AD: Ranee Flynn P: Hans Gissinger CW: Suzanne Hooper DF: Elizabeth Arden

SHISEIDO

Packaging; 1992; CD, AD: Shuichi Ikeda D: Aoshi Kudo

(bottom) Poster; 1986; CD: Isamu Hanauchi CD, AD, P, CW: Serge Lutens AD: Toshio Yamagata
D: Yoshikatsu Okamoto P: Seiichi Nakamura

SHISEIDO

COLOR REFLECTS
BY SERGE LUTENS

MAKEUP AUTUMN-WINTER 1986

Shiseido

Country of original launch: Japan
Year of launch: 1872
Coverage: cosmetics / perfume

A comprehensive range of products designed and developed for
domestic and overseas markets, and promoted on the basis of
meticulous marketing strategies.

資生堂では、国内ブランド・海外向けブランドを問わず、
厳密なマーケティング戦略に基づいた明確な宣伝活動・
イメージクリエーションを遂行している。

Shiseido 189

Poster; 1991; CD, AD: Toshio Yamagata CD, AD, P, CW: Serge Lutens
AD, D: Yutaka Kobayashi D: Hiromi Motoyama P: Seiichi Nakamura

Poster; 1987; CD: Isamu Hanauchi CD, AD, P, CW: Serge Lutens AD: Toshio Yamagata
D: Yoshikatsu Okamoto P: Seiichi Nakamura

190 Shiseido

Poster; 1988; CD: Isamu Hanauchi CD, AD, P, CW: Serge Lutens AD: Toshio Yamagata
D: Yoshikatsu Okamoto P: Seiichi Nakamura

Poster; 1993; CD, AD: Toshio Yamagata CD, AD, P, CW: Serge Lutens
D: Hiromi Motoyama / Takayasu Yamada P: Seiichi Nakamura

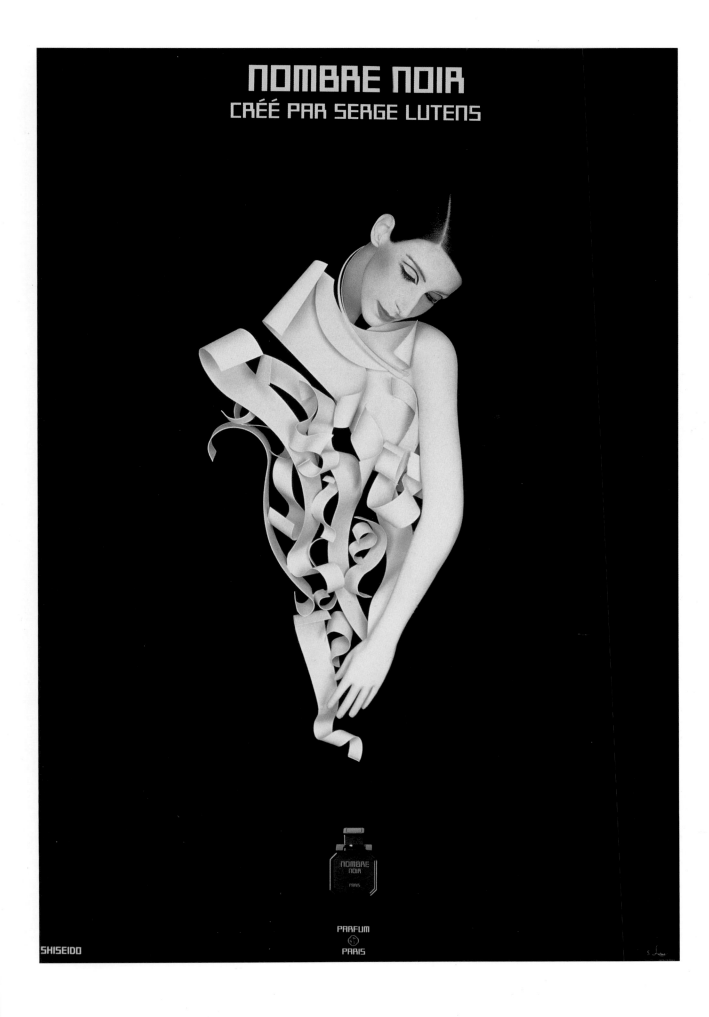

Poster; 1982; CD, P, CW: Serge Lutens AD: Ikuo Amano D: Toshio Yamagata

Brochure; 1992; CD: Toshio Yamagata AD, D: Yutaka Kobayashi P, CW: Serge Lutens P: Seiichi Nakamura I: Christian Jean

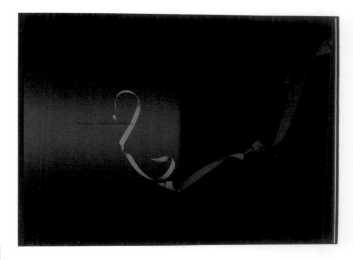

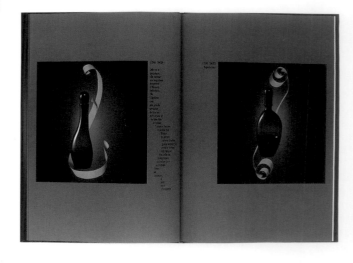

 192 Shiseido

Chant du Cœur

シャンデュクール そして、心が歌いだす

Bottle design by Angela Cummings   Fragrance by Edouard Fléchier   Produced by SHISEIDO

Magazine ad; 1992; CD: Hiroshi Tanaka AD, D: Yoshikatsu Okamoto P: Nick Night CW: Shoko Yoshida

Shiseido + 193

Packaging; 1992; CD, D: Shuichi Ikeda AD, D: Angela Cummings

Poster; 1992; CD, AD, D: Ikuo Amano P: Noriaki Yokosuka CW: Takeo Nagasawa

Packaging; 1987; CD, AD, D: Shunsaku Sugiura D: Izumi Matsumoto

194   Shiseido

Packaging; 1992; CD, AD: Shuichi Ikeda D: Aoshi Kudo

女を、微妙にする香り

Poster; 1990; CD: Reikichi Nakayama AD, D: Kazuo Yasuhara P: Noriaki Yokosuka CW: Kan Obata

Shiseido ✚ 195

SONIA RYKIEL

PARFUMS - BEAUTÉ

Sonia Rykiel Parfums Beauté

Designer: Sonia Rykiel
Country of original launch: France
Year of launch: 1993 (Le Parfum)
Coverage: Perfume

Created to match Sonia's ideal of a perfume that accentuates the myriad strands of a woman's nature without hampering their diversity, "Le Parfum" is a mysterious yet superb blend of several contrasting fragrances.

多種の個性を "統一" させるのではなく、それぞれの良さを
活かし "共存" させる。そんなソニアの意志が反映された香水
"Le Parfum" は、いくつもの相反する香りが見事に
調和された、ミステリアスな一品である。

Sonia Rykiel Parfums Beauté + 197

CHANEL

CHANEL

Country of original launch: France
Year of launch: 1921 (No.5)
Coverage: Cosmetics / perfume

Coco Chanel launched her first perfume - No.5 - in 1921, and more than half a century later, women continue to be enchanted by its mystical fragrance.

1921年にココ・シャネルが初めて作り出した香水 ── それが "No.5"。半世紀以上を過ぎた現代でも、その神秘的な香りは変わらずに女性たちを魅了しつづけている。

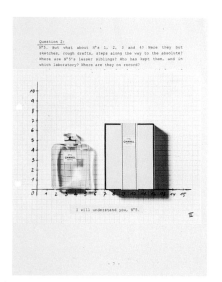

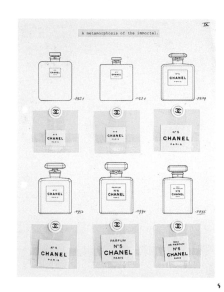

Brochure; 1993; CD, AD, D: Alain Lachartre CW: Pascal Avot DF: Vue Sur La Ville

Sem and Warhol.
The history of art is also the history of N°5.

Clients & Submittors

abahouse • devinette
Client: **Abahouse International Co.Ltd.**
Submittor: **Abahouse International Co.Ltd.**

agete
Client: **Sazaby Inc.**
Submittor: **Sazaby Inc.**

CHANEL
Client: **Chanel**
Submittor: **Vue Sur La Ville**

Cimarron
Client: **Saez Merino France**
Submittor: **Saez Merino France**

Corinne Cobson
Client: **Quartier Général**
Submittor: **Quartier Général**

Daniel Jasiak
Client: **Daniel Jasiak composition indéfinie:**
Submittors: **Daniel Jasiak composition indéfinie: / Collaboration Co.Ltd.**

Diesel
Client: **Diesel S.p.A.**
Submittor: **Baderman**

Elizabeth Arden
Client: **Elizabeth Arden**
Submittor: **Elizabeth Arden**

Esprit
Client: **Esprit de Corps.**
Submittors: **Erin Lorch / Andrew Hoyne Design**

Fiorucci
Client: **Fiorucci SRL**
Submittor: **Fiorucci SRL**

202

Clients & Submittors

Fire & Ice
Client: **Willy Bogner**
Submittor: **Instant. Design Limited**

5351 Pour Les Hommes et Les Femmes
Client: **Abahouse International Co.Ltd.**
Submittor: **Abahouse International Co.Ltd.**

French Connection
Client: **French Connection**
Submittor: **French Connection**

Ghost
Client: **Ghost Ltd.**
Submittor: **Ghost Ltd.**

Guess?
Client: **Guess?, Inc.**
Submittor: **Guess?, Inc.**

Hiroko Koshino
Client: **Hiroko Koshino Design Office Inc.**
Submittor: **Mizutani Studio**

Hysteric Glamour
Client: **Ozone Community Corporation**
Submittor: **Ozone Community Corporation**

I.S.
Client: **Issey Miyake Inc.**
Submittor: **Issey Miyake Inc.**

Ipsa
Client: **Ipsa Co.Ltd.**
Submittor: **Ipsa Co.Ltd.**

Katharine Hamnett London
Client: **Katharine Hamnett Ltd.**
Submittors: **Katharine Hamnett Ltd. / Itochu Fashion System Co.Ltd. / G.C.O. Co.Ltd.**

Kesalan Patharan
Client: **Kesalan Patharan**
Submittor: **Mizutani Studio**

Krizia
Client: **Krizia S.p.A.**
Submittor: **SPAZIO Institute for Advanced Thinking Inc.**

Lolita Lempicka
Client: **Leslie Léonor International**
Submittor: **Leslie Léonor International**

Moschino
Client: **Moonshadow S.p.A.**
Submittor: **Sushi Co.Ltd.**

Ozone Community
Client: **Ozone Community Corporation**
Submittor: **Ozone Community Corporation**

Paul Smith
Client: **Paul Smith Ltd.**
Submittors: **Paul Smith Japan / Joi'x Corporation**

R. Newbold
Client: **Paul Smith Ltd.**
Submittors: **Paul Smith Japan / Joi'x Corporation**

Red or Dead
Client: **Red or Dead Limited**
Submittor: **Red or Dead Limited**

Rykiel Homme
Client: **Sonia Rykiel CDM**
Submittors: **Sonia Rykiel CDM / Sonia Rykiel Japon K.K.**

Shiseido
Client: **Shiseido Co.Ltd.**
Submittor: **Shiseido Co.Ltd.**

Clients & Submittors

Shu Uemura
Client: **Shu Uemura Cosmetics Inc.**
Submittor: **Nakatsuka Daisuke Inc.**

SISLEY
Client: **Benetton Group S.p.A.**
Submittor: **United Agency K.K.**

Sonia Rykiel
Client: **Sonia Rykiel CDM**
Submittors: **Sonia Rykiel CDM / Sonia Rykiel Japon K.K.**

Sonia Rykiel Parfums Beauté
Client: **Sonia Rykiel CDM**
Submittors: **Sonia Rykiel CDM / Sonia Rykiel Japon K.K.**

Studio-V
Client: **Vivid Co.Ltd.**
Submittor: **Vivid Co.Ltd.**

Takéo Kikuchi
Client: **World Co.Ltd.**
Submittor: **World Co.Ltd.**

United Colors of Benetton
Client: **Benetton Group S.p.A.**
Submittor: **United Agency K.K.**

VIVAYOU
Client: **Sanei · International Co.Ltd.**
Submittor: **Sanei · International Co.Ltd.**

Yoshiki Hishinuma
Client: **Hishinuma Associates Co.Ltd.**
Submittor: **Hishinuma Associates Co.Ltd.**

4 °C
Client: **F.D.C. Products Co.Ltd.**
Submittor: **F.D.C. Products Co.Ltd.**

FASHION & COSMETICS GRAPHICS

Art Director / Designer
Miyuki Kawanabe

Editor
Ayako Aoyama

Business Manager
Masato Ieshiro

Photographer
Kuniharu Fujimoto

Coordinators
Chizuko Gilmore (San Francisco)
Sarah Phillips (London)
Christine Oyama (Paris)

English Translator & Consultant
Sue Herbert

Publisher
Shingo Miyoshi

1995年7月9日 初版第1版発行

発行所 ピエ・ブックス
〒170 東京都豊島区駒込4-14-6 ビラフェニックス301
TEL: 03-3949-5010 FAX: 03-3949-5650

製版 (株)サンニチ印刷
〒151 東京都渋谷区代々木2-10-8 ケイアイ新宿ビル
TEL: 03-3374-6241 FAX: 03-3374-6252

印刷・製本 エバーベスト・プリンティング(株)
Printed and Bound by Everbest Printing Co.Ltd.
Ko Fai Industrial Building, Block C5, 10th Floor
7 Ko Fai Road, Yau Tong, Kowloon, Hong Kong
TEL: 852-2727-4433 FAX: 852-2772-7908

ISBN4-938586-50-9 C3070 P16000E

THE P·I·E COLLECTION

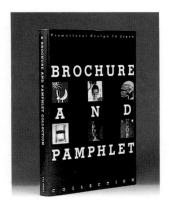

BROCHURE & PAMPHLET COLLECTION 1
Pages: 224(144 in color) ￥15,000
業種別カタログ・コレクション
Here are hundreds of the best brochures and pamphlets from Japan.
This collection will make a valuable sourcebook for anyone involved in corporate identity advertising and graphic design.

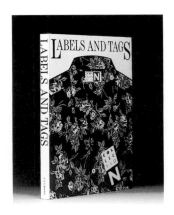

LABELS AND TAGS
Pages: 224(192 in color) ￥15,000
ファッションのラベル＆タグ・コレクション
Over 1,600 garment labels representing 450 brands produced in Japan are included in this full-color collection.

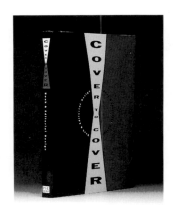

COVER TO COVER
Pages: 240(176 in color) ￥17,000
世界のブック＆エディトリアル・デザイン
The latest trends in book and magazine design are illustrated with over 1,000 creative works by international firms.

BUSINESS STATIONERY GRAPHICS 1
Pages: 224(192 in color) ￥15,000
世界のレターヘッド・コレクション
Creatively designed letterheads, business cards, memo pads, and other business forms and documents are included this international collection.

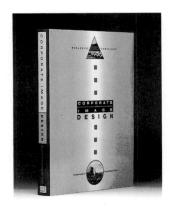

CORPORATE IMAGE DESIGN
Pages: 336(272 in color) ￥16,000
世界の業種別CI・ロゴマーク
This collection presents the best corporate identity projects from around the world. Creative and effective designs from top international firms are featured in this valuable source book.

POSTCARD GRAPHICS 3
Pages: 232(208 in color) ￥16,000
世界の業種別ポストカード・コレクション
Volume 3 in the series presents more than 1,200 promotional postcards in dazzling full color. Top designers from the world over have contributed to this useful image bank of ideas.

GRAPHIC BEAT London / Tokyo 1 & 2
Pages: 224(208 in color) ￥16,000
音楽とグラフィックのコラボレーション
1,500 music-related graphic works from 29 of the hottest designers in Tokyo and London. Features Malcolm Garrett, Russell Miles, Tadanori Yokoo, Neville Brody, Vaughn Oliver and others.

BUSINESS CARD GRAPHICS 2
Pages: 224(192 in color) ￥16,000
世界の名刺＆ショップカード、第2弾
This latest collection presents 1,000 creative cards from international designers. Features hundreds of cards used in creative fields such as graphic design and architecture.

T-SHIRT GRAPHICS
Pages: 224(192 in color) ￥16,000
世界のTシャツ・グラフィックス
This unique collection showcases 700 wonderfully creative T-Shirt designs from the world's premier design centers. Grouped according to theme, categories include sports, casual, designer and promotional shirts among others.

DIAGRAM GRAPHICS
Pages: 224(192 in color) ￥16,000
世界のダイアグラム・デザインの集大成
Hundreds of unique and lucid diagrams, charts, graphs, maps and technical illustrations from leading international design firms. Variety of media represented including computer graphics.

SPECIAL EVENT GRAPHICS
Pages: 224(192 in color) ￥16,000
世界のイベント・グラフィックス特集
This innovative collection features design elements from concerts, festivals, fashion shows, symposiums and more.
International works include posters, tickets, flyers, invitations and various premiers.

RETAIL IDENTITY GRAPHICS
Pages: 208(176 in color) ￥14,800
世界のショップ・グラフィックス
This visually exciting collection showcases the identity design campaigns of restaurants, bars, shops and various other retailers. Wide variety of pieces are featured including business cards, signs, menus, bags and hundreds more.

PACKAGING DESIGN & GRAPHICS 1
Pages: 224(192 in color) ¥16,000
世界の業種別パッケージ・デザイン
An international collection featuring 400 creative and exciting package designs from renowned designers.

ADVERTISING GREETING CARDS 3
Pages: 224(176 in color) ¥16,000
世界のダイレクトメール集大成、第3弾
The best-selling series continues with this collection of elegantly designed advertising pieces from a wide variety of categories. This exciting image bank of ideas will interest all graphic designers and direct mail specialists.

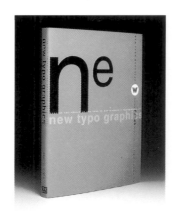

NEW TYPO GRAPHICS
Pages: 224(192 in color) ¥16,000
世界の最新タイポグラフィ・コレクション
New and innovative typographical works gathered from top designers around the world. A wide variety of type applications are shown including posters, brochures, CD jackets, calendars, book designs and more.

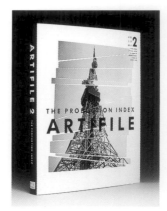

The Production Index ARTIFILE 2
Pages: 244(240 in color) ¥13,500
活躍中！最新プロダクション年鑑、第2弾
A design showcase featuring the best works from 115 graphic design studios, photographers, and creators in Japan. Works shown include print advertisements, corporate identity pieces, commercial photography and illustration.

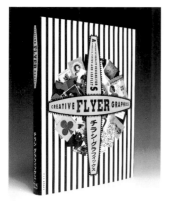

CREATIVE FLYER GRAPHICS
Pages: 224(176 in color) ¥16,000
チラシ・グラフィックス
Features about 500 rigorously screened flyers and leaflets. You see what superior graphics can accomplish on a single sheet of paper. This is an invaluable reference to all your advertising production for years to come.

1, 2 & 3 COLOR GRAPHICS
Pages: 208(Full Color) ¥16,000
1・2・3色 グラフィックス
See about 300 samples of 1,2 & 3 color artwork that are so expressive they often surpass the impact of full 4 color reproductions. This is a very important book that will expand the possibilities of your design works in the future.

LABELS AND TAGS 2
Pages: 224(192 in color) ¥16,000
世界のラベル＆タグ・コレクション　2
This long-awaited second volume features 1500 samples representing 400 top name-brands from around the world.

BROCHURE DESIGN FORUM 2
Pages: 224(176 in color) ¥16,000
世界の最新カタログ・コレクション　2
Features 70 businesses and 250 reproductions for a complete overview of the latest and best in brochure design.

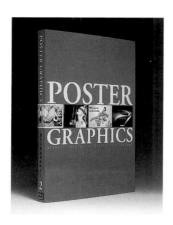

POSTER GRAPHICS 2
Pages: 256(192 in color) ¥17,000
業種別世界のポスター集大成
700 posters from the top creators in Japan and abroad are showcased in this book - classified by business. This invaluable reference makes it easy to compare design trends among various industries and corporations.

BUSINESS STATIONERY GRAPHICS 2
Pages: 224(192 in color) ¥16,000
世界の業種別レターヘッド・コレクション、第2弾
The second volume in our popular "Business Stationery Graphics" series. This publication focuses on letterheads, envelopes and business cards, all classified by business. This collection will serve artists and business people well.

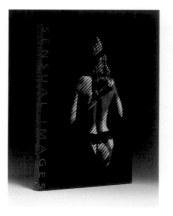

SENSUAL IMAGES
Pages: 208(98 in color) ¥4,800
世界の官能フォト傑作集
We selected the best sensual works of 100 photographers from all over the world. The result is 200 sensual images concentrated in this volume. Page after page of photos that will quicken your pulse and stimulate your fantasies!

BROCHURE & PAMPHLET COLLECTION 3
Pages: 224(176 in color) ¥16,000
好評！業種別カタログ・コレクション、第3弾
The third volume in "Brochure & Pamphlet" series. Sixteen types of businesses are represented through artwork that really sell. This book conveys a sense of what's happening now in the catalogue design scene. A must for all creators.

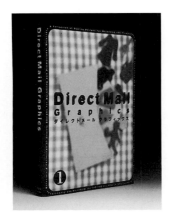

DIRECT MAIL GRAPHICS 1
Pages: 224(176 in color) ￥16,000
衣・食・住のセールスDM特集
The long-awaited design collection featuring direct mailers with outstanding sales impact and quality design. 350 of the best pieces, classified into 100 business categories. A veritable textbook of current direct marketing design.

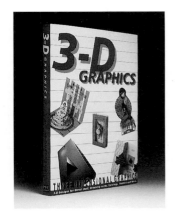

3-D GRAPHICS
Pages: 224(192 in color) ￥16,000
3-D・グラフィックスの大百科
300 works that demonstrate the best possibilities of 3-D graphic methods, including DMs, catalogues, posters, POPs and more. The volume is a virtual encyclopedia of 3-D graphics.

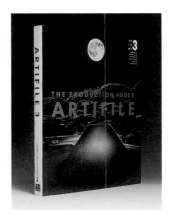

The Production Index ARTIFILE 3
Pages: 224(Full color) ￥13,500
活躍中！最新プロダクション年鑑、第3弾
Contributors are 116 top production companies and artists. See the artwork and read insightful messages from the creators.

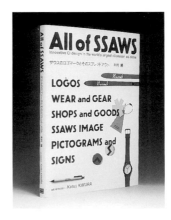

ALL OF SSAWS
Pages: 120(Full color) ￥8,800
ザウスのCI、アプリケーション & グッズ
The graphics of SSAWS - the world's No.1 all-season ski dome is showcased in this publication; everything from CI and rental wear to notions and signs. This is the CI concept of the future - design that changes, evolves and propagates freely.

TYPO-DIRECTION IN JAPAN 5
Pages: 254(183 in color) ￥17,000
年鑑　日本のタイポディレクション'93
314 award-winning typographic works from around the world are shown in this book. It includes recent masterpieces by eminent art directors and designers as well as powerful works by up-and-comoing designers.

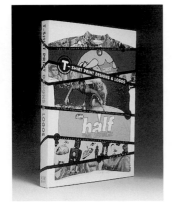

T-SHIRT PRINT DESIGN & LOGOS
Pages: 224(192 in color) ￥16,000
世界のTシャツ・プリントデザイン&ロゴ
Volume 2 of our popular "T-shirt Graphics" series. In this publication, 800 designs for T-shirt graphics, including many trademarks and logotypes are showcased. The world's top fashion makers are featured.

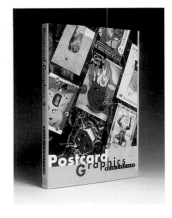

POSTCARD GRAPHICS 4
Pages: 224(192 in color) ￥16,000
世界の業種別ポストカード・コレクション
Our popular Postcard Graphics series has been revamped for Postcard Graphics Vol.4. This new-look volume showcases approximately 1,000 varied examples selected from the world's best and ranging from direct mail to private greeting cards.

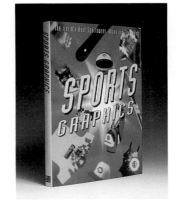

SPORTS GRAPHICS
Pages: 224(192 in color) ￥16,000
世界のスポーツ用品グラフィックス
An up-beat collection of 1,000 sporting-goods graphics from all around the world. This book features a variety of different goods, including uniforms, bags, shoes and equipment, and covers all sorts of sports: soccer, basketball, skiing, surfing and many, many more.

The Paris Collections / INVITATION CARDS
Pages: 200(192 in color) ￥16,000
パリ・コレクションの招待状グラフィックス
The Paris Collections are renowned for style and sophistication. Individual designers present their collections, and this volume features about 430 invitation cards for these shows, each mirroring the prestige and originality of the fashion house, and together encapsulating the glamour of Paris.

COMPANY BROCHURE COLLECTION
Pages: 224(192 in color) ￥16,000
業種別（会社・学校・施設）案内グラフィックス
Private companies, schools and leisure facilities - 220 informative brochures and guides, classified by type of business, from all sorts of enterprises and facilities throughout Japan. A fascinating and useful catalogue of imaginative layouts combined with effective design.

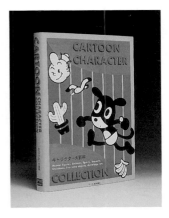

CARTOON CHARACTER COLLECTION
Pages: 480(B/W) ￥9,800
キャラクター大百科
A selection of 5,500 carefully chosen, quality cartoon drawings from the most successful illustrators in the business. Conveniently classified, the drawings cover everything from animals and natural scenery to food, sports and seasonal images. An encyclopedic collection and a useful source book.

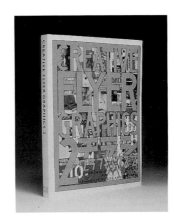

CREATIVE FLYER GRAPHICS 2
Pages: 224(208 in color) ￥16,000
世界のチラシ・グラフィックス 2
This follow-up volume presents around 600 different flyers and leaflets promoting just about everything! From information on arts and music to advertising of food, consumer products and package tours, this selection demonstrates the power-packed design features of promotional flyers.

カタログ・新刊のご案内について

総合カタログ、新刊案内をご希望の方は、はさみ込みのアンケートはがきを
ご返送いただくか、90円切手同封の上、ピエ・ブックス宛お申し込み下さい。

**CATALOGUES ET INFORMATIONS SUR LES NOUVELLES
PUBLICATIONS**

Si vous désirez recevoir un exemplaire gratuit de notre catalogue général
ou des détails sur nos nouvelles publications, veuillez compléter la carte
réponse incluse et nous la retourner par courrierou par fax.

CATALOGUES AND INFORMATION ON NEW PUBLICATIONS

If you would like to receive a free copy of our general catalogue or
details of our new publications, please fill out the enclosed postcard
and return it to us by mail or fax.

CATALOGE UND INFORMATIONEN ÜBER NEUE TITLE

Wenn Sie unseren Gesamtkatalog oder Detailinformationen über
unsere neuen Titel wünschen, fullen Sie bitte die beigefügte Postkarte
aus und schicken Sie sie uns per Post oder Fax.

ピエ・ブックス
〒170 東京都豊島区駒込 4-14-6-301
TEL: 03-3949-5010 FAX: 03-3949-5650

P·I·E BOOKS
#301, 4-14-6, Komagome, Toshima-ku, Tokyo 170 JAPAN
TEL: 03-3949-5010 FAX: 03-3949-5650